S0-BIO-627

Real Estate Dictionary

Pocket Guide for Professionals

Charles Jacobus
Houston Community College

Nora Olmos
Houston Community College

SOUTH-WESTERN
CENGAGE Learning

Australia • Brazil • Japan • Korea • Mexico • Singapore • Spain
United Kingdom • United States

SOUTH-WESTERN
CENGAGE Learning

Real Estate Dictionary: A Pocket Guide for Professionals
Charles Jacobus and Nora Olmos

Vice President/Editorial Director: Jack W. Calhoun

Vice President/Editor-in-Chief: Dave Shaut

Director of Publishing, Real Estate, and Professional
    Certification: Scott Person

Developmental Editor: Sara Froelicher

Marketing Manager: Mark Linton

Production Manager: Barbara Fuller Jacobsen

Manufacturing Coordinator: Charlene Taylor

Internal Design: Hyde Park Publishing Services

Production: Hyde Park Publishing Services

Cover Design: Rick Moore

Cover Image: © PhotoDisc, Inc.

For product information and technology assistance,
contact us at **Cengage Learning Customer &
Sales Support, 1-800-354-9706**

For permission to use material from this text or product,
submit all requests online at **www.cengage.com/permissions**
Further permissions questions can be e-mailed to
permissionrequest@cengage.com

Library of Congress Control Number: 2003113847

ISBN-13: 978-0-324-20518-3

ISBN-10: 0-324-20518-X

South-Western Cengage Learning
5191 Natorp Boulevard, Mason, OH 45040, USA

Cengage Learning is a leading provider of customized learning
solutions with office locations around the globe, including Singapore,
the United Kingdom, Australia, Mexico, Brazil, and Japan. Locate your
local office at **www.cengage.com/global**

Cengage Learning products are represented in Canada by
Nelson Education, Ltd.

To learn more about South-Western, visit
www.cengage.com/southwestern

Purchase any of our products at your local college store or at our
preferred online store **www.cengagebrain.com**

Printed in the United States of America
3 4 5 6 13 12 11 10

Contents

Appendices

A

"A" paper – a loan rating given based on excellent credit; usually with a FICO score of 620 or higher.

abandonment – the voluntary surrender or relinquishing of possession of real property without vesting this interest in another person, homestead.

abatement – property tax exemptions used and property tax reductions granted to attract industry.

absolute deed – a deed used in lieu of a mortgage, also called a deed absolute.

absorption field – a system of narrow trenches through which the discharge from a septic tank infiltrates into the surrounding soil.

absorption rate – the rate in which a liquid or mixture of liquid and gases is drawn into the pores of a porous solid material.

abstract – a summary of all recorded documents affecting title to a given parcel of land.

abstract of judgment – a document filed for record pursuant to a judgment by a court of competent jurisdiction that creates a general lien on all the judgment debtor's real estate in that county.

abstract of title – a complete historical summary of all recorded documents affecting the title of a property.

abstractor (conveyancer) – an expert in title search and abstract preparation.

abut – to be adjacent; touch or border.

Accelerated Cost Recovery System (ACRS) – a rapid depreciation write-off method.

accelerated depreciation – any method of depreciation that achieves a faster rate of depreciation than straight-line.

acceleration clause – See *alienation clause.*

acceptance – the act of a person to whom a thing is offered or tendered by another, whereby he receives the thing with the intention of retaining it, such intention being evidenced by a sufficient act.

access right – the right to use.

accession – the addition to land by man or nature.

accord – agreement or consent.

accounts payable – a liability to a creditor for purchases of goods or services.

accounts receivable – a claim against a debtor for the sale of goods or services.

Accredited Resident Manager (ARM) – professional designation for property managers.

accretion – the process of land buildup by waterborne rock, sand, and soil.

accrued interest – accumulated or earned interest over a period of time.

acknowledgment – a formal declaration before authorized officials by a person that he or she, in fact, did sign the document.

acoustical ceiling – a ceiling of fibrous tiles, panels, or other sound-deadening material.

acquisition – to come into possession or ownership.

acquisition loan – a loan for acquiring or gaining possession.

acre – a unit of land measurement that contains 4,840 square yards or 43,560 square feet.

ACRS – See *Accelerated Cost Recovery System.*

Act of God – an inevitable act by the forces of nature.

action to quiet title – action for land ownership.

active investor – an investor who actively participates in the property invested in.

actual age – See *effective age*.

actual cash value – the new price less accumulated depreciation.

actual eviction – the landlord serves notice on the tenant to comply with the lease contract or vacate.

actual notice – knowledge one has gained based on what has been actually seen, heard, read, or observed.

ad valorem tax – tax levied according to the value of one's property; the more valuable the property, the higher the tax, and vice versa.

ad valorem tax lien – a lien for real property taxes.

ADA – See *Americans with Disabilities Act*.

adaptation – the manner in which certain items of personalty are conformed to or made especially for a parcel of real estate.

addendums – See *rider*.

addition – See *modification*.

additional property clause – provision in a mortgage instrument providing for the mortgage to serve as additional security for any additional property to be acquired that will be attached to the real estate.

adjacent – See *abut*.

adjustable rate mortgage (ARM) – a mortgage loan on which the interest rate rises and falls with changes in prevailing rates.

adjusted basis – the original basis plus the cost of capital improvements less any allowance for depreciation.

adjusted market price – the value of a comparable property after adjustments have been made for differences between it and the subject property.

adjusted sales price – the sales price of a property less commissions, fix-up, and closing costs.

adjustment period – the amount of time that elapses between adjustments of an adjustable mortgage loan.

adjustments – changes.

administrator – a person appointed by a court to carry out the instructions found in a will (male).

administratrix – a person appointed by a court to carry out the instructions found in a will (feminine).

advance cost listing – a listing wherein the seller is charged for the out-of-pocket costs of marketing the property.

advance fee listing – a listing wherein the broker charges an hourly fee and for the out-of-pocket expenses.

adverse land use – See *adverse possession*.

adverse possession – acquisition of real property through prolonged and unauthorized occupation of another's land.

affidavit – a written or printed declaration or statement of facts made voluntarily, and confirmed by the oath or affirmation of the party making it, taken before an officer having authority to administer such an oath.

affordable housing loan – an umbrella term that covers many slightly different loans that target first-time home buyers and low to moderate-income borrowers.

a-frame – a house with a triangle front and back and a roof that slopes to the ground forming the sides of the house. It is shaped like a capital A.

a-frame

After Acquired Title Doctrine – a doctrine under which title acquired by a grantor, who previously attempted to convey title to land that he did not in fact own, inures automatically to the benefit of prior grantees.

agency – a relationship created when one person (the principal) delegates to another person (the agent) the right to act on the principal's behalf.

agency by estoppel – relationship that results when a principal fails to maintain due diligence over his agent and the agent exercises powers not granted to him.

agency by ratification – the establishment of an agency relationship by the principal after the agency objective has been accomplished.

agency coupled with an interest – an irrevocable agency in which the agent has an interest in the property as part or all of his compensation.

agency disclosure – a form disclosing to the buyer that the broker represents the seller in all transactions unless the buyer chooses to hire that broker for representation. The disclosure must be made very early in the transaction, usually at the point of first significant contact with the buyer (i.e., obtaining specific information from the buyer as to his or her financial capacity, as to the property he or she wants to purchase, or other information that may be deemed confidential. Similar forms exist if a situation develops where the buyer decides that he or she wants representation from the broker or if the broker represents the buyer and the buyer requests that the broker submit an offer on one of his or her own listings.

agent – the person empowered to act by and on behalf of the principal. See also *agency; broker*.

agreement of sale – See *installment contract*.

air lot – a designated airspace over a parcel of land.

air right – the right to occupy and use the airspace above the surface of a parcel of land.

air space – commonly referred to as the "unit" in condominium ownership.

AIREA – See *American Institute of Real Estate Appraisers, The*.

alienation clause – a clause in a note or mortgage that gives the lender the right to call the entire loan balance due if the property is sold or otherwise conveyed.

alienation of title – a change in ownership of any kind.

allodial system – one in which individuals are given the right to own land.

all-risks policy – all perils, except those excluded in writing, are covered.

alluvion – the increase of land when waterborne soil is gradually deposited.

amendatory language – government-required clauses in FHA and VA contracts.

amendment – the method used to change a zoning ordinance.

American Institute of Real Estate Appraisers, The (AIREA) – a professional organization of appraisers. Unified in 1991 with the Society of Real Estate Appraisers (SREA) and renamed The Appraisal Institute; it is considered to provide the most highly respected designations in the industry.

Americans with Disabilities Act (ADA) – a federal law giving disabled individuals the right of access to commercial facilities open to the public.

amortization term – the amount of time it takes to amortize a debt.

amortize – to liquidate a debt by making periodic payments.

amortized loan – a loan requiring periodic payments that include both interest and partial repayment of principal.

amount financed – amount of credit provided to the borrower.

amount realized – selling price less selling expenses.

amperage – the amount of current or electricity flowing through a wire.

analysis – the act or process of providing information, recommendations, and/or conclusions on problems.

anchor post – component of a tieback used to support a wood retaining wall; the anchor post is attached perpendicularly to the back of the wall.

annexation – the attachment of personal property to real estate; municipality's right to extend jurisdiction over contiguous property.

annual percentage rate (APR) – a uniform measure of the cost of credit that includes interest, discount points, and loan fees.

annuity – a series of periodic payments; for example, money received in a long-term lease.

anticipation, principle of – what a person will pay for a property depends on the expected benefits from the property in the future.

antideficiency laws – See *deficiency judgment*

antitrust laws – federal and state laws prohibiting monopolies and restraint of trade.

apartment – in condominium housing, an enclosed space consisting of one or more rooms occupying all or part of a floor in a building of one or more floors or stories regardless of whether it be designated for a residence or an office, for the operation of any industry, business, or for any type of independent use, provided it has a direct exit to a thoroughfare or to a given space leading to a thoroughfare.

apartment locators – firms that specialize in finding rental units for tenants.

apportionment – See *cost approach*, *income approach*, and *market comparison approach*.

appraisal – an estimate of value.

appraisal letter – a valuation report in the form of a business letter.

Appraisal Review Board – the appeals board for a taxpayer who chooses to protest the appraisal of his or her property.

appraise – to estimate the value of something.

appraised value – the appraiser's best *estimate* of the subject property's worth.

appraiser – one who is licensed or certified by their respective states based on examination, education, and experience requirement to estimate the value of something.

appreciation – an increase in property value.

appropriation process – the enactment of a taxing body's budget and sources of money into law.

appurtenance – right or privilege or improvement that belongs to and passes with land but is not necessarily a part of the land.

appurtenant – adjoining.

APR – See *annual percentage rate*.

aquifer – below ground-level rock bed over which water flows.

architecture – the profession of designing buildings, communities, and other artificial constructions.

ARM – See *Accredited Resident Manager* and *adjustable rate mortgage*.

asbestos – a fibrous material found in rocks and soil.

ash pit – a cavity underneath the firebox that is used as a receptacle for ashes and is accessible through a cleanout door.

ash pit cleanout door – a metal door located at the base of the chimney that leads to the ash pit.

as-is – said of property offered for sale in its present condition with no guarantee or warranty of quality provided by the seller.

assemblage – the process of combining two or more parcels into one.

assessed value – a value placed on a property for the purpose of taxation.

assessment – See *assessed value*.

assessment appeal board – local governmental body that hears and rules on property owner complaints of overassessment.

assessment district – See *improvement district*.

assessment roll – a list or book, open for public inspection, that shows assessed values for all lands and buildings in a taxing district.

assessor – a public official who evaluates property for the purpose of taxation.

assessor's map – one that shows assessor parcel numbers for all land parcels in a taxing district.

assessor's parcel number – a system for assigning numbers to land parcels to aid in property tax assessment and collection.

asset integrated mortgage – a mortgage designed to create a savings from the down payment.

assign – to transfer to another one's rights under a contract.

assignee – one to whom a right or property is transferred.

assignment – the total transfer of one's rights under a contract to another.

assignment of rents – establishes the lender's right to take possession and collect rents in the event of loan default.

assignor – one who assigns a right, title, or interest to another.

associate broker – a broker that is associated with a designated broker.

associate licensee – a salesperson that is associated with a broker.

association – a not-for-profit organization that can own property and transact business in its own name.

association dues – fees paid by a condominium or planned unit development owner to the owner's association for upkeep of the common elements.

assumable loan – an existing loan that can be assumed by a creditworthy individual.

assume the loan – the buyer obligates himself or herself to repay an existing loan as a condition of the sale.

assumption – the buyer is obligated to repay an existing loan as a condition of the sale.

at-risk – the amount of money an investor stands to lose.

attachment – the act or process of taking, apprehending, or seizing persons or property by virtue of a writ or other judicial order and bringing same into the custody of the court. This is often done to compel an appearance or furnish security for debts or costs to satisfy a judgment that a plaintiff may obtain. See also *rider*.

attorney-in-fact – one who is authorized by another to act in his or her place.

auction – the sale of real estate through a bidding process.

automated underwriting systems – computerized systems for loan approval communication between a loan originator and the investor.

automatic form of trusteeship – the trustee is named in the deed of trust, but is not personally notified of the appointment until called upon.

avulsion – sudden loss or gain of land because of water or a shift in a riverbed that has been used as a boundary.

B

back-end ratio – a loan qualifying ratio based on total living expenses.

backfill – earth filled in around a foundation wall to replace earth removed for construction of the foundation.

backflow preventer – keeps water from backing up in a water supply or drainage system.

back-up offer – a purchase contract that goes into effect when a pending contract fails.

balance sheet – a statement of the financial position of a business on a specified date.

balloon framing – uses a single system of wall studs that run from the foundation through to the first and second floors to the ceiling support.

balloon loan – a loan in which the final payment is larger than the preceding payments.

balloon payment – the name given to the final payment of a balloon loan.

baluster – pole or post that runs from the stair handrail vertically to the tread.

bank – (1) commercial lending institution; (2) the shore of a river or stream.

bankruptcy – insolvency, ruin and failure.

bare title – See *naked title*.

bargain and sale deed – a deed that contains no covenants, but does imply that the grantor owns the property being conveyed.

bargain brokers – a term that refers to real estate brokers who charge less than most competing brokers in their area.

base industry – an industry that produces goods or services for export from the region.

base line – a set of imaginary lines running east and west in locating and describing land under the rectangular survey method.

base rent – the minimum rent paid in a percentage lease.

basis – used in calculating income taxes. See also *tax basis*.

beam – a straight horizontal structural member whose main purpose is to carry transverse loads.

bearing wall – supports the ceiling or the roof and includes the outside wall frame.

bearings – directional designations used in metes-and-bounds legal description.

bedrock – the hard, solid rock formation at or below the surface of the earth.

before-and-after method – an appraisal technique used when a part of the property has been condemned, as under the right of eminent domain.

benchmark – a reference point of known location and elevation.

beneficial interest – a unit of ownership in a real estate investment trust.

beneficiary – one for whose benefit a trust is created; the lender in a deed of trust arrangement.

beneficiary statement – a lienholder's statement as to the unpaid balance on a trust deed note.

bequest – personal property received under a will.

biannual – occurring twice a year.

biennial – taking place once every two years.

bilateral contract – results when a promise is exchanged for a promise.

bill of sale – a written agreement by which one person transfers his personal property to another.

binder – a short purchase contract used to secure a real estate transaction until a more formal contract can be signed.

biweekly mortgage loan – a mortgage loan that is paid every two weeks.

blanket mortgage – a mortgage that is secured by more than one real property.

blended-rate loan – a refinancing plan that combines the interest rate on an existing mortgage loan with current rates.

blind nailing – a method of nailing in which the head of the nail is countersunk, then covered with putty to be hidden from view.

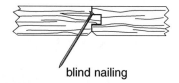

blind nailing

blind pool – an investment pool wherein properties are purchased after investors have already invested their money.

block – See *recorded plat*.

blockbusting – the illegal practice of inducing panic selling in a neighborhood for financial gain.

blue-sky law – state law designed to protect persons from buying into dubious investment schemes.

board of adjustment – a board appointed by a local revenue body allowed to make special exceptions to the terms of the zoning ordinance in harmony with the general purpose and intent and in accordance with the general or specific rules therein contained. The board of adjustment also serves as an appellate board for any person aggrieved by a previous zoning decision or decision of any administrative officer of the municipality.

board of directors – the governing body of a corporation.

board of equalization – a governmental body that reviews property tax assessment procedures.

boards – lumber less than 2 in. (50.8 mm) thick and 1 in (25.4 mm) or more wide.

boiler plate – the detailed standard wording of a contract.

boilers – used to transfer heat from a fuel source to a fluid, such as water, and are constructed from cast iron, steel, or copper.

BOMI – See *Building Owners and Managers Institute*.

bona fide – authentic or genuine.

bona fide purchaser – a purchaser who acquires property without notice of any defects in title.

boot – additional compensation paid in a property exchange.

borrower's points – charges in one-percent units of a loan, paid by a borrower to obtain a loan.

boundaries – something that indicates bounds or limits.

boycotting – refusing to do business with another to eliminate competition.

branch circuit wiring – wiring that goes from the main panel board through the walls of the building to the switches and outlets.

breach of contract – failure without legal excuse to perform as required by a contract.

bridge loan – the principal loan given to bridge or connect with the construction loan.

British Thermal Unit (BTU) – a measure of heat energy required to raise the temperature of one pound of water by one degree Fahrenheit.

broad form (HO-2) – an insurance policy that covers a large number of named perils.

broad market – one wherein many buyers and many sellers are in the market at the same time.

broker – a person or legal entity licensed to act independently in conducting a real estate brokerage business.

brokerage – an agreement in which a client pays a broker to carry out a real estate transaction.

BTU – See *British Thermal Unit*.

budget mortgage – features loan payments that include principal, interest, taxes, and insurance (often called PITI).

buffer zone – a strip of land that separates one land use from another.

building codes – local and state laws that set minimum construction standards.

building envelope – the materials that enclose the interior and through which heating, cooling, and fresh air passes.

Building Owners and Managers Institute (BOMI) – professional designation for property managers.

building permit – permission from the appropriate local government authority to construct or renovate any type of property.

building setback – See *setback requirements*.

bullet loan – commonly known as a balloon mortgage with severe prepayment penalties.

bundle of rights theory – the theory that describes the legal rights an owner has over his property.

bus bars – conductors on the main panel board that provide electrical connections for fuses or circuit breakers.

business day – a week day during business hours in which business transactions occur.

business homestead – a place or property used to exercise the calling of a business that is exempt from execution by force creditor by operation of law.

buy-down – a cash payment to a lender that creates lower monthly mortgage payments for a period of time for the buyer.

buyer's broker – a real estate licensee who represents the buyer rather than the seller.

buyer's market – one with few buyers and many sellers.

buyer's walk-through – a final inspection just prior to settlement.

bylaws – rules that govern how an owners' property association will be run.

C

cadastral map – a graphic map indicating location, boundaries and property lines.

call – (1) a lender's right to require early repayment of the loan balance; (2) the right to buy at present price and terms for a fixed period of time. See also *alienation clause*.

cancellation rights – right of the buyer or seller to nullify or void; express intent to withdraw from a transaction.

canons – standards of conduct.

cap rate – See *capitalization rate*.

capital asset – property that is not stock-in-trade (inventory) used in a trade or business of a kind subject to depreciation, as well as notes in accounts receivable acquired in the course of the trade or business.

capital gain – the gain (profit) on the sale of an appreciated asset.

capital gains tax treatment – a special tax rate allowed by the Internal Revenue Code for profits on the sale of capital assets.

capitalization rate – a rate that expresses profit as a percentage of the invested capital.

capitalize – to convert future income to current value.

carpenter ant – a type of insect that eats wood.

carpenter bee – a type of insect that eats wood.

carryback financing – an owner financed second mortgage.

case law – individual court decisions.

casement window – a window that opens from the side on hinges.

casement window

cash equivalent value – the value of something when converted into cash.

cash flow – the number of dollars remaining each year after collecting rents and paying operating expenses and mortgage payments.

cash value – the amount of money a policyholder would receive if the policy were surrendered to an insurance company, or the amount the policyholder could borrow against the policy.

cashier's check – a check drawn by a bank on its own funds and signed by its cashier.

cash-on-cash – the cash flow produced by a property divided by the amount of cash necessary to purchase it.

casing – the material that surrounds the window on the inside.

catalytic combustor – a ceramic, round, square, or rectangular insert with numerous small channels, or tubes, running through it that increase combustion activity.

caveat emptor – let the buyer beware.

CD – See *certificate of deposit.*

cemetery lot – a lot in a cemetery, graveyard, or burial ground.

ceramic tile – a type of tile that is either glazed or unglazed and s used for flooring, countertops, and exterior applications. Ceramic tiles made for the floor may have textured surfaces to avoid slippage.

CERCLA – See *Comprehensive Environmental Response, Compensation, and Liability Act of 1980.*

certificate of deposit (CD) – a saver's commitment to leave money on deposit for a specific period of time.

certificate of limited partnership – a certificate that must be filed with the Secretary of State that discloses certain facts concerning the limited partnership.

certificate of occupancy – a government-issued document that states a structure meets local zoning and building code requirements and is ready for use.

certificate of reasonable value (CRV) – a certificate that reflects the estimated value of the property as determined by the Veteran's Administration staff appraiser.

certificate of reduction – a document prepared by a lender showing the remaining balance on an existing loan.

certificate of sale – a certificate the high bidder receives entitling him to a referee's or sheriff's deed if no redemption is made.

certificate of title – an opinion by an attorney as to who owns a parcel of land; a Torrens certificate that shows ownership as recognized by a court of law.

certified property manager (CPM) – professional designation for property manager.

cession deed – a deed that conveys street rights to a county or municipality.

cesspool – a pit (sometimes lined with plastic) composed of stones and gravel through which raw sewage collects; it's a health and safety hazard and a code violation.

chain – a surveyor's measurement that is 66 feet long.

chain of title – the linkage of property ownership that connects the present owner to the original source of title.

characteristics of land – fixity, immobility, indestructibility, modification, nonhomogeneity, scarcity, and situs.

characteristics of value – demand, scarcity, transferability, and utility.

charges – in judicial parliaments, the instructions a judge gives to the jury.

chattel – an article of personal or moveable property.

chattel mortgage – a pledge of personal property to secure a note.

check – a 24-by-24 mile area created by guide meridians and correction lines in the rectangular survey system.

checklist report – a systemized itemization of the various components of a property that is organized into sections that allow the inspector to check off inspected property components and comment on any specific problems.

circuit – path that electricity travels.

circuit breakers – trip and switch off the electrical power for a given circuit if the current increases beyond the capacity of the system.

circuit court of civil appeals – the appellate court having jurisdiction in the federal court system to which appeals from the district court may be made.

clay tile – a flooring material used in many homes because of its durability. Tiles are classified as either quarry tile, paver tile, or ceramic tile.

Clayton Antitrust Act – federal statute that specifically prohibits price discrimination, exclusive dealing arrangements, certain corporate acquisitions of stock, and interlocking directorates.

cleanout – a pipe fitted with a removable plug to assist in dislodging a pipe obstruction.

clear title – a clean title without claims, liens or encumbrances.

client – the broker's principal.

CLO – See *computerized loan origination*.

closed-end mortgage – a mortgage that cannot extend additional funds to the borrower.

closing – See *title closing*.

closing costs – the costs paid by the buyer and the seller when finalizing a real estate transaction.

closing date – the day on which the title closing is completed.

closing into escrow – a closing where all parties sign their documents and entrust them to the escrow agent.

closing meeting – a meeting at which the buyer pays for the property, receives a deed to it, and all other matters pertaining to the sale are concluded.

closing statement – See *settlement statement*.

cloud on title – any claim, lien, or encumbrance that impairs title to property.

code of ethics – articles that pertain to the REALTOR®'s relation to clients, other real estate agents, and the public.

codicil – a written supplement or amendment to an existing will.

COFI – See *Cost of Fund Index*.

co-insurance – the insurer and the insured share the insurance risk; calculated on the policy amount and the percent of the actual insured values.

cold call – soliciting clients by telephone.

COLI – See *Cost of Living Index*.

collateral – security pledged for the payment of a loan.

collusion – a conspiracy for fraudulent purposes.

color of title – some plausible, but not completely clear-cut indication of ownership rights.

commercial bank – a bank specializing in checking and savings accounts and short-term loans.

commingling of funds – the mixing of clients' or customers' funds with an agent's personal funds.

commission – compensation for brokers and salespersons.

commitment fee – a fee paid to a lender to commit funds that would be advanced at a future date.

common elements – those parts of a condominium in which each unit owner holds an undivided interest.

common law – law that develops from custom and usage over long periods of time.

common law dedication – results when a landowner's acts or words show intent to convey land to the government.

common wall – See *party wall easement*.

common-law marriage – a marriage that becomes operative by operation of law rather than one of formal decree or ceremony.

community property – property co-ownership wherein husband and wife are treated as equal partners with each owning a one-half interest.

Community Reinvestment Act – federal statute encouraging federally regulated lenders to encourage their participation in low-income areas.

comparables– properties similar to the subject property that are used to estimate the value of the subject property.

comparative market analysis – See *market comparison approach*.

compensation – for brokers and salespersons.

competent party – persons considered legally capable of entering into a binding contract.

competitive market analysis – a method of valuing homes that looks at recent home sales and at homes presently on the market plus homes that were listed but did not sell.

complete appraisal – the act or process of estimating value without invoking the Departure Provision.

compound interest – the interest paid on both the principal and on the accrued interest.

Comprehensive Environmental Response, Compensation, and Liability Act of 1980 (CERCLA) – the law that was enacted by congress in 1980 in response to the environmental and public health hazards imposed by improper disposition of hazardous waste.

comprehensive plan – See *master plan*.

compressor – an air conditioner component that creates a flow of refrigerant from one part of the system to the other.

computerized loan origination (CLO) – originating loans through the use of a networked computer system.

concession – See *rent concession*.

concrete – a solid, hard material produced by combining portland cement, aggregates, sand, and water and sometimes admixtures.

concrete block – a hollow brick of concrete manufactured to be used in building walls and raised foundations.

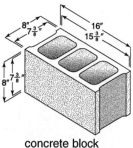

concrete block

concurrent jurisdiction – the jurisdiction of several different courts, each authorized to deal with the same subject matter.

concurrent ownership – ownership by two or more persons at the same time.

condemnation – the legal action of taking property under the power of eminent domain.

condenser – an air conditioner component that liquefies the refrigerant gas by cooling it.

conditional sales contract – See *installment contract.*

conditional-use permit – allows a land use that does not conform with existing zoning.

condominium – individual ownership of single units or apartments in a multiple-unit structure or structures with common elements.

condominium association – a homeowner association for condominium owners.

condominium declaration – a document that converts a given parcel of land into a condominium subdivision.

condominium project – a real estate condominium project; a plan or project whereby four or more apartments, rooms, office spaces, or other units in existing or proposed buildings or structures are offered or proposed to be offered for sale.

condominium records – records in county clerk's office to record condominium declaration.

condominium subdivision – a document that converts a parcel of land into a number of individual separate property estates.

condominium unit owner's form (HO-6) – a policy that covers additions or alterations not covered by the association's policy.

conductors – wires that electricity moves through; good conductors have little resistance to the flow of electricity.

conduit – a steel or plastic tube through which electrical wires are run.

confirmed – when the assessment roll is approved.

conforming loan – a conventional loan that follows Fannie Mae and Freddie Mac residential loan requirements.

conformity, principle of – maximum value is realized when there is a reasonable degree of homogeneity in a neighborhood.

connection line – a survey line that connects a surveyor's monument with a permanent reference mark.

consequential damages – an award to a property owner whose land is not taken but which suffers because of a nearby public land use.

consideration – an act or promise given in exchange for something; anything of value, such as money or property, given to induce another to enter into a contract.

construction mortgages – short-term loans made during the construction of a building, but prior to the permanent loan.

constructive eviction – tenant breaks the lease because the landlord does not keep the premises habitable.

constructive notice – notice given by the public records and by visible possession, coupled with the legal presumption that all persons are thereby notified.

Consumer Price Index (CPI) – an index in the changes of the cost and services to a typical consumer based on the costs of the same items in a previous period.

contingency – dependence on the fulfillment of a condition.

contingency clause – a clause expressing a possibility conditional on something uncertain.

contingent remainder – a remainder limited so as to depend upon an event or condition that may never happen to be performed until after termination of the preceding estate.

contingent sale – a sale based on the conditional possibility of another sale.

continuing education – additional education required to renew one's license.

contour lines – lines on a topographic map that connect points having the same elevation.

contour map – a map that shows land elevations.

contract – a legally enforceable agreement to do (or not to do) a particular thing.

contract for deed – See *installment or land contract*.

contract for sale – an enforceable sale agreement between two or more parties.

contract rent – the amount of money that the tenant must pay the landlord for the use of the premise as specified in the lease contract. See also *economic rent*.

contract zoning – an agreement by a governing body to enact a change in land-use classification in exchange for certain concessions to be granted by the developer or applicant.

contractor – See *independent contractor*.

contractual intent – precludes jokes or jests from becoming valid contracts.

contractual liens – liens that arise as a result of a contract between the parties.

contribution, principle of: we should invest dollars whenever they will return to us more than $1 of value and should stop when each dollar invested returns less than $1 in value.

control joints – vertical spaces in the brick wall joints that allow for the expansion and contraction of the brick and mortar.

convector – heat-emitting unit in which heat is produced by the movement of air around a metal surface.

conventional loan – real estate loan that is not insured by the FHA or guaranteed by the VA.

conversion – an agent's personal use of money belonging to others.

convertible ARM – an adjusted rate mortgage that can be converted into a fixed rate mortgage.

convey – to transfer the title of a property.

conveyance – the transfer of property from one person to another.

conveyance tax – a fee or tax on deeds and other documents payable at the time of recordation.

co-op – See *cooperative*.

cooperating broker – a broker who, acting as an agent of the listing broker, procures a buyer.

cooperative – land and building owned or leased by a corporation, which in turn leases space to its shareholders; ownership of shares in a cooperative venture that entitles the owner to use, rent, or sell a specific apartment unit.

cooperators – individual shareholders in a cooperative.

co-owner – in condominiums, a person, firm, corporation, partnership, association, trust, or other legal entity, or any combination thereof, who owns an apartment or apartments within the condominium project.

corner lot – a lot that fronts on two or more streets.

cornice – trim piece for the eave.

corporate charter – the official document indicating the existence of the corporation as authorized by the Secretary of State.

corporation – a business owned by stockholders; a legal entity recognized by law with tax rates separate from individual income tax rates.

corporeal – material, tangible.

corpus – trust assets, the body of a trust.

correction deed – a document used to correct an error in a previously recorded deed.

correction lines – survey lines used to correct for the earth's curvature.

correlation process – a step in an appraisal wherein the appraiser weights the comparables.

cosigner – a joint signer of a negotiable instrument.

cost approach – land value plus current construction costs minus depreciation.

cost handbook – books containing construction cost information.

Cost of Fund Index (COFI) – an index used to determine interest rate changes for adjustable-rate mortgages.

Cost of Living Index (COLI) – an index in the changes of costs that include food, clothing, transportation, personal and medical care, and other costs periodically determined by the Department of Labor.

cost-push inflation – higher prices due to increased costs of labor and supplies.

co-tenancy – joint tenancy.

council of co-owners – all of the co-owners of a condominium project.

counterflashing – a second layer of flashing.

counteroffer – an offer made in response to an offer.

county – a territorial division of and unit of local government.

county court – court whose jurisdiction is in the county in which it is situated but has a ceiling on the dollar amount that can be litigated within its jurisdiction.

covenant – a written agreement or promise.

covenant against encumbrances – grantor warrants that there are no encumbrances other than those stated in the deed.

covenant against removal – borrower promises not to remove or demolish any buildings or improvements.

covenant of further assurance – grantor will procure and deliver to the grantee any subsequent documents necessary to make good the grantee's title.

covenant of good repair – the borrower is required to keep the mortgaged property in good condition.

covenant of insurance – the borrower is required to carry adequate insurance against damage or destruction of the mortgaged property.

covenant of preservation and maintenance – See *covenant of good repair*.

covenant of quiet enjoyment – grantor warrants that the grantee will not be disturbed.

covenant of seizin – grantor warrants that he or she is the owner.

covenant to pay taxes – the borrower agrees to pay the taxes on the mortgaged property even though the title may be technically with the lender.

covenants, conditions, and restrictions – privately imposed deed and lease restrictions.

CPI – See *Consumer Price Index.*

CPM – See *certified property manager.*

credit – the reputation of a person or firm for the paying of bills when due.

credit rating – an indication of the risk involved when giving credit to a person or firm.

credit report – a report reflecting the credit-worthiness of a borrower by showing past credit history.

credit scoring – a number that assesses a borrower's credit history and current credit based on credit bureau reports.

creditor – a person or firm to whom money is due.

creosote – a black tar-like substance that builds up inside the chimney through normal use.

cricket – composed of metal flashing, it prevents snow and ice from building up against the chimney.

CRV – See *certificate of reasonable value.*

cul de sac – a street closed at one end with a circular turnaround.

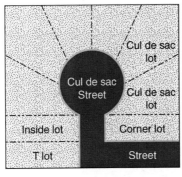

cul de sac

curable depreciation – depreciation that can be fixed at reasonable cost.

curb – a low wall of wood or masonry extending above the level of the roof and surrounding an opening in the roof.

curtesy – the legal right of a widower to a portion of his deceased wife's real property.

customer – a person with whom the broker and principal negotiate; third party.

D

damages – the estimated money equivalent for loss or injury sustained.

damper – a plate or valve that closes the fireplace flue when the fireplace is not in use, preventing heat loss.

datum – any point, line, or surface from which a distance, vertical height, or depth is measured.

deadman – component of a tieback used to support a wood retaining wall; the deadman is positioned parallel to the wall and perpendicular to the anchor post.

dealer property – real property held for other than personal use.

debit – to charge as a debt.

debt – an obligation to be repaid by a borrower.

debt service – the amount of money necessary to meet the periodic payment of principal and interest.

debtor – a person or company in debt.

debt-to-income ratio – the percentage of debt in relation to income.

decedent – a deceased person.

decibel – a unit for measuring sound energy or power.

declaration – See *master deed*.

dedication – the voluntary conveyance of private land to the public.

deed – a written document that when properly executed and delivered conveys title to land.

deed as security – a deed given to secure a loan and treated as a mortgage.

deed covenants – See *deed restrictions*.

deed in lieu of foreclosure – a voluntary act by both borrower and lender.

deed of confirmation – See *correction deed*.

deed of trust (*also called* trust deed) – a document that conveys legal title to a neutral third party as security for a debt.

deed restrictions – provisions placed in deeds to control how future landowners may or may not use the property.

deed tax – a tax on conveyances of real estate.

deed without warranties – See *bargain and sale deed*.

default – failure to perform a legal duty, such as a failure to carry out the terms of a contract.

defeasance clause – a mortgage clause that states the mortgage is defeated if the accompanying note is repaid on time.

deferred interest mortgage – a mortgage with a monthly payment that is less than the amount required to pay the note rate; the unpaid interest is deferred by adding it to the loan balance.

deficiency judgment – a judgment against a borrower if the foreclosure sale does not bring enough to pay the balance owed.

delayed exchange – a nonsimultaneous tax-deferred trade.

delinquent loan – a loan wherein the borrower is behind in his or her payments.

delivery – the final and absolute transfer of a deed, properly executed, to the grantee, or to some person for his use, in such manner that it cannot be recalled by the grantor.

delivery and acceptance – title passes when the grantor delivers the deed and the grantee accepts it.

demand – a need or desire coupled with the purchasing power to fill it.

demand-pull inflation – higher prices due to buyers bidding against each other.

demise – the conveyance of an estate under lease.

density – the average number of inhabitants and dwellings per unit of area.

Department of Housing and Urban Development (HUD) – government agency responsible for creating opportunities for home-ownership, providing assistance for low-income persons, working to create, rehabilitate and maintain the nation's affordable housing, enforcing housing laws, helping homeless, spurring economic growth in distressed neighborhoods, and helping local communities meet their development needs.

deposit – earnest money tendered in conjunction with an offer to purchase real property.

deposit receipt – receipt given for a deposit that accompanies an offer to purchase; also refers to a purchase contract that includes a deposit receipt.

depreciation – loss in value due to deterioration and obsolescence.

dereliction – the process whereby dry land is permanently exposed by a gradually receding waterline.

descent and distribution – heirship.

designated broker – the principal broker in a real estate establishment.

developer – an individual who adds to the value of land by erecting improvements upon the land.

devise – the transfer of real property by means of a will.

devisee – one who receives real property under a will.

devisor – one who grants real property under a will.

diminishing marginal returns, principle of – we should invest dollars whenever they will return to us more than $1 of value and should stop when each dollar invested returns less than $1 in value.

disability – incapacity, a physical or mental handicap.

disaffirm – revoke.

disclaimer – is appended to the home inspection report and documents the scope of the inspection and specifically indicates which items are omitted from the report, including opinions about the structure and design, building code compliance, and environmental problems.

disclosure – something disclosed, to make known.

disclosure statement – a form generally furnished to the seller by a real estate agent, the form asks the seller to disclose detailed information regarding the property.

discount – a payment of interest in advance; prepaid interest.

discount broker – a full-service broker who charges less than the prevailing commission rates in that community.

discount points – charges made by lenders to adjust the effective rate of interest on a loan.

discrimination – unequal treatment of a potential home buyer or renter based on his or her race, color, religion, sex or age, as defined by the Fair Housing Act of 1986.

disintermediation – the movement of money out of savings accounts and into corporate and government debt instruments; the result created when lenders are required to pay high rates of interest for deposits while receiving long-term income from low-interest rate mortgage loans.

distributees – those designated by law to receive the property of the deceased when there is no will.

distribution box – a part of a septic system that distributes the flow from the septic tank evenly to the absorption field or seepage pits.

district courts – state courts whose jurisdiction is within a statutorily defined district that is generally larger than that of the county. Its jurisdiction is, for the most part, similar to that of county courts, but there is no dollar limit on the amount that can be litigated.

divided agency – See *dual agency*.

doctrine of capture – a legal philosophy that states the first to use water has a prior right to its use.

doctrine of merger – a doctrine by which the earnest money contract in a real estate transaction is extinguished by absorption into the deed or other instruments passed at closing. See also *easements*.

doctrine of prior appropriation – a legal philosophy that allows a first user to continue diverting water.

documentary tax – a fee or tax on deeds and other documents payable at the time of recordation.

doing business as (d/b/a) – a sole proprietorship that operates under a name other than the owner's.

dollars per hundred – property tax rate.

dollars per thousand – property tax rate.

domicile – a place of residence; a permanent legal residence.

dominant estate – an parcel of land to which a servitude or easement is attached. See also *subsurface rights*.

dominant tenement – See *dominant estate*.

donee – a person who receives a gift.

donor – a person who makes a gift.

double top plate – used to tie walls together and provide additional support for the ceiling and roof system. It is made up of two or more structural timbers that are bolted together with a metal plate sandwiched between for additional strength.

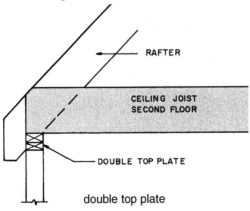

double top plate

dower – the legal right of a widow to a portion of her deceased husband's real property.

down payment – an initial partial payment at the time of purchase.

downside risk – the possibility that an investor will lose his money in an investment.

downzoning – rezoning of land from a higher-density use to a lower-density use.

dragnet clause – See *future advance clause*.

drainage – the land's ability to draw off surface water.

dry closing – a closing that is essentially complete except for disbursement of funds and delivery of documents.

dry rot – a decay of wood that usually results from alternate soaking and drying over a long period.

dual agency – agency in which the licensee represents both the buyer and the seller.

dual contract – two contracts written with different teams and financing in an attempt to obtain a larger loan; a fraudulent practice.

duct – a hollow tube through which air is circulated.

due date – a contract or payment date; a deadline.

due diligence – care in performing one's duties for a client.

due process of law – law in its regular course of administration through courts of justice.

due-on-sale clause – See *alienation clause*.

dummy – See *straw man*.

duplex – a house or an apartment with two separate living units.

durable power of attorney – power of attorney that does not lapse because of the passage of time unless a time limitation is specifically stated in the instrument creating it.

duress – the application of force to obtain an agreement.

dwelling – place of residence.

E

E&O insurance – See *Errors and Omission insurance.*

earnest money – money that accompanies an offer to purchase as evidence of good faith.

earnest money contract – a contract for the sale or purchase of real estate in which the purchaser is required to tender earnest money to evidence his good faith in completing contractual obligations.

easement – the right of another to use or have access to land belonging to another; also called *right-of-way.*

easement appurtenant – an easement that runs with the land.

easement by necessity – an easement created by law usually for the right to travel to a landlocked parcel of land.

easement by prescription – acquisition of an easement by prolonged use.

easement in gross – an easement given to a person or business to use or travel over the land of another.

eave – the lowest part of the roof that projects beyond the walls of the structure.

economic base – the ability of a region to export goods and services to other regions and receive money in return.

economic life – the period over which a property may be profitably utilized.

economic obsolescence – loss of value due to external forces or events.

economic rent – the amount of rent a property can command in the open market.

effective age – the apparent age of a building, not the actual age or chronological age.

effective interest rate – the true rate of return; the actual return or yield to the investor.

effective yield – a return on investment calculation that considers the price paid, the time held, and the interest rate.

efflorescence – white stains often observed on the foundation wall or floor slab that are caused by masonry mineral salts combining with water as it penetrates through the floor or wall.

egress – exit; the right to leave a tract of land.

EIR – See *Environmental Impact Report.*

elastic pressure cells – a type of well-water storage includes cells that have a capacity of about three gallons. A cell is composed of a metal cylinder with an elastic liner on the inside. As the pump delivers water under pressure to the cell, the elastic liner is compressed as the cylinder is filled. Then, when a faucet is turned on, the water is forced out of the cell by the pressure provided by the expanding liner. See also *well-water storage tank.*

electric current – the flow of electrons along a conductor such as a copper wire.

electromagnetic field – occurs anytime electricity flows through a wire; there are two separate fields—an electric field and a magnetic field.

elevations – views of vertical planes, showing components in their vertical relationship, viewed perpendicularly from a selected vertical plane.

eligible taxpayers – taxpayers who have the ability to offset their active income with passive losses.

emblement – annual planting that requires cultivation.

eminent domain – the right of government to take privately held land for public use, provided fair compensation is paid.

employee – one who works for an employer who has the right to control and direct the employee as to the details and means by which a result is to be accomplished.

employment contract – formalizes the working arrangement, between broker and principal (listing) and between broker and salesperson.

encroachment – trespass on the land of another as a result of an intrusion by some structure or other object.

encumbrance – any impediment to a clear title, such as a lien, lease, or easement.

endorsement – a policy modification.

entailments – a limitation by which property is different from the course it would take if the creator of the entailment would have allowed the general succession to his heirs in accordance with law. The creator of an entailment normally limits or abridges the fee to certain classes of issue instead of to all his descendants generally.

entitlement – the loan amount a veteran is entitled to or eligible to borrow.

entry and possession – the borrower moves out and the lender moves in, which is witnessed and recorded.

Environmental Impact Report (EIR) – report that contains information regarding the effect of a proposed project on the environment of an area.

Environmental Protection Agency (EPA) – the federal governmental agency in charge of protecting the environment.

eo instanti – Latin term meaning "immediately."

EPA – See *Environmental Protection Agency*.

Equal Credit Opportunity Act – federal law that provides for equal credit to borrowers.

equitable lien – a lien that exists in equity. It is a mere floating and ineffective equity until such time as a judgment or decree is rendered actually subjecting property to the payment of the debt or claim.

equitable maxim – generally accepted statement of equitable rules that are considered to be conclusions of common sense and reason.

equitable mortgage – a written agreement that is considered to be a mortgage in its intent even though it may not follow the usual mortgage wording.

equitable title – the right to demand that title be conveyed upon payment of the purchase price; the beneficial interest of one person in real property although legal title is vested in another.

equity – (1) the market value of a property less the debt against it; (2) a doctrine of fairness and honesty between two persons whose rights or claims are in conflict.

equity build-up – the increase of one's equity in a property due to mortgage balance reduction and price appreciation.

equity courts – courts that administer justice according to a system of equity.

equity mortgage – a line of credit made against the equity in a person's home.

equity of redemption – the borrower's right prior to foreclosure to repay the balance due on a delinquent mortgage loan.

equity sharing – an agreement whereby a party providing financing gets a portion of the ownership.

erosion – the wearing away of land by water, wind, or other processes of nature.

errors and omission (E&O) insurance – designed to pay legal costs and judgments against persons in business.

escalation clause – provision in a lease for upward and downward rent adjustments.

escheat – the power of the state to take title to property left by a person who has died and has no legal heirs.

escrow – the deposit of instruments and/or funds with instruction to a third party to carry out the provisions of an agreement or contract.

escrow account – a separate account for holding clients' and customers' money. See also *impound account*.

escrow agent – disinterested third party placed in charge of an escrow, typically in a closing.

escrow agreement – an agreement where the seller assigns his interest in the contract to the qualified intermediary.

escrow closing – the deposit of documents and funds with a neutral third party along with instructions as to how to conduct the closing.

escrow company – a firm that specializes in handling the closing of a transaction.

estate – the extent of one's legal interest or rights in land; the extent of one's real and personal property in general.

estate at sufferance – one that comes into the possession of land by lawful title but holds over by wrongful possession after the termination of his interest.

estate at will – a leasehold estate that can be terminated by a lessor or lessee at any time.

estate for life – See *freehold estate*.

estate for years – an estate for one who has a temporary use and possession for lands and tenements not his own, by virtue of a lease or demise granted to him by the owner, for a determinate period of time, as for a year or a fixed number of years.

estate from period to period – a tenancy in which one holds lands or tenements under the demise of another where no certain term has been mentioned but a periodic rental has been reserved, normally a rental from year to year or semiannually, which may be automatically renewed at the end of the term.

estate in land – the degree, quality, nature, and extent of interest that a person has in real property.

estate in reversion – the right to future enjoyment of property presently possessed or occupied by another.

estate in severalty – See *severalty ownership*.

estate tax value – the value that federal and state taxation authorities establish for a deceased person's property.

estoppel – an inconsistent position, attitude, or course of conduct that may not be adopted to the loss or injury of another, easements.

estoppel certificate – a document in which a borrower verifies the amount still owed and the interest rate.

et al – a Latin term used in real estate to express "and others."

ethics – See *code of ethics*.

evaporator – an air conditioner component that takes heat from the air surrounding it and brings it to the refrigerant.

eviction – the act of depriving a person of a possession of land that he has held pursuant to the judgment of the court of competent jurisdiction.

evidence of title – being able to prove interest in title.

exclusive agency – an agency relationship where only buyers or sellers will be represented.

exclusive agency listing – a contract giving one agent the right to sell property for a specified time, but reserving the right of the owner to sell the property himself without the payment of the commission.

exclusive authority to purchase – listing utilized by buyer's brokers.

exclusive right to sell – a listing agreement that gives the broker the right to collect a commission no matter who sells the property during the listing period.

execute – the process of completing, performing, or carrying out something.

executed – performance has taken place.

executed contract – one in which nothing remains to be done by either party and the transaction is completed at the moment when the arrangement is made, as when an article is sold and delivered, and payment therefore is made on the spot.

execution – a legal order directing an official to enforce a judgment against the property of a debtor, normally through a "writ of execution."

executive director – the person in charge of real estate regulation in a state.

executor – a person (masculine) named in a will to carry out its instructions and requests.

executor's deed – a deed used to convey the real property of a deceased person.

executory – in the process of being completed.

executory contract – a contract in which some future act is to be done.

executrix – a person (feminine) named in a will to carry out its instructions and requests.

export industry – See *base industry*.

express agency – an agency relationship that is created when a principal employs a real estate agent to act for him.

express contract – a contract made orally or in writing.

express grant – method of creating an easement.

extension springs – generally mounted just above the horizontal track of the garage door, they provide lifting power by stretching (extending).

external obsolescence – conditions that reduce the value of the property caused by forces outside of the property.

extraterritorial jurisdiction – the unincorporated area, not a part of any other city, that is contiguous to the corporate limits to the city.

F

face amount – the dollar amount of insurance coverage.

face value – apparent value.

facilitator – a licensee who has no fiduciary responsibility as no agency has been formed.

failure of purpose – a method for termination of easements.

Fair Credit Reporting Act – federal law giving an individual the right to inspect his or her file with the credit bureau and correct any errors.

fair market value – See *market value*.

Fair, Isaac Company (FICO) – a credit scoring company that began in 1956 in San Rafael, CA. See also *credit rating* and *credit scoring*.

faithful performance – a requirement that an agent obey all legal instructions given by the principal.

false advertising – making misrepresentations in advertising.

familial status – one or more individuals under the age of 18 who are domiciled with a parent or other person having legal custody.

Fannie Mae – See *Federal National Mortgage Association*.

fascia – the area of material facing the outer edge of the soffit.

FDIC – See *Federal Deposit Insurance Corporation*.

Federal Agricultural Mortgage Corporation (Farmer Mac) – provides a secondary mortgage market for farm real estate loans.

Federal clauses – refers to government-required clauses in real estate contracts.

Federal Deposit Insurance Corporation (FDIC) – a federal agency that insures deposits in commercial banks.

Federal Discount Rate – federal reduced rate.

federal district courts – courts of the United States, each having a territorial jurisdiction over a district, which may include a whole state or only a part of the state.

Federal Fair Housing Act – a federal law that prohibits discrimination in housing based on race, color, religion, sex, handicap, familial status, and national origin.

Federal Home Loan Bank Board (FHLBB) – the former name for the regulatory and supervisory agency for federally chartered savings institutions; this agency is now called Office of Thrift Supervision.

Federal Home Loan Banks – twelve regional banks that supply loans for savings associations.

Federal Home Loan Mortgage Corporation (FHLMC or "Freddie Mac") – agency providing a secondary mortgage market facility for savings and loan associations.

Federal Housing Administration (FHA) – government agency that insures lenders against losses due to nonrepayment.

Federal National Mortgage Association (FNMA) – provides a secondary market for real estate loans.

federal questions – a case arising under the Constitution of the United States, acts of Congress, or treaties involving an interpretation and application. The jurisdiction of federal questions is given to the federal courts.

Federal Reserve Board – the governing board of the nation's central bank.

Federal Reserve System ("the Fed") – the federal central banking system responsible for the nation's monetary policy by regulating the supply of money and interest rates.

Federal Savings and Loan (S&L) Associations – also known as thrifts, offer savings deposits and mortgage loans; at one time, S&Ls made the majority of the residential loans in the country.

Federal Savings and Loan Insurance Corporation (FSLIC) – now defunct; deposit insured Savings and Loan Associations.

Federal tax lien – a federal tax charge against a property.

fee – See *fee simple*.

fee ownership – full ownership.

fee simple conditional – a fee estate that calls for a happening of some event or the performance of some act before the transfer is complete.

fee simple defeasible – a fee estate that can be defeated if a certain condition occurs.

fee simple determinable – a fee estate limited by the happening of a specified event.

fee simple estate – an estate in which the owner is entitled to the entire property with unconditional power or disposition during his lifetime and descending to his heirs and legal representatives upon his death intestate. It is the largest, most complete bundle of rights one can hold in land ownership.

fee simple subject to condition subsequent – a fee estate in which the grantor has the right to terminate it.

fee tail – specially named heirs are to inherit the estate. If such heirs are not available, the estate reverts to the grantor or to his or her heirs.

felt paper – a roofing material placed on top of the plywood or particleboard decking of the roof system.

feudal system – all land ownership rests in the name of the king.

FHA – See *Federal Housing Administration*.

FHLBB – See *Federal Home Loan Bank Board*.

FHLMC – See *Federal Home Loan Mortgage Corporation*.

fiat money – money created by the government, printing press money.

FICO – See *Fair, Isaac Company*.

fictional depreciation – depreciation deductions as allowed by tax law.

fictitious business name – a name other than the owner's that is used to operate a business.

fiduciary – a person in a position of trust, responsibility, and confidence for another, such as a broker for a client.

fiduciary relationship – when an agency is created.

filler industry – See *service industry*.

finance charge – the total dollar amount the credit will cost the borrower over the life of the loan.

financial institution – any intermediary such as a commercial bank that accepts deposits for the purpose of lending those deposits for a return of profit.

Financial Institutions Reform, Recovery, and Enforcement Act (FIRREA) – the act that established mandatory requirements for real estate appraisals, appraiser qualifications, changed banking practices and mortgage lending.

financial leverage – See *leverage*.

financial liability – the amount of money one can lose, one's risk exposure; investing.

financing – obtaining funds for a purchase.

financing statement – evidence of indebtedness secured by chattel and filed on record in the county courthouse or Secretary of State's office.

finder's fee – a finder's fee paid to an individual for bringing together the parties to a transaction.

finish floor – the flooring that is left exposed to view.

fire insurance – dwelling coverage which is the basic insurance policy or the minimum homeowner's coverage.

fire wall – a construction of noncombustible materials that subdivides a building or separates adjoining buildings to retard the spread of fire.

fire-stop – a member used to close openings between studs, joists, and other members to retard the spread of fire through openings between them.

FIRREA – See *Financial Institution's Reform, Recovery, and Enforcement Act*.

first mortgage – the mortgage loan with priority over any other loan(s) on the property for repayment in the event of foreclosure.

first refusal – See *right of first refusal*.

fiscal year – a yearly period established for accounting purposes.

fixed cost – See *sunk cost*.

fixed rate loan – a loan in which the interest rate will not change during the life of the loan.

fixed-pane windows – do not open or close (e.g., picture window or variations of the bay window).

fixity – refers to the fact that land and buildings require long periods of time to pay for themselves.

fixture – an item of personalty that has been attached to real estate such that it becomes real estate.

fixture filing – financing statement evidencing the fact that the chattel is or is to become fixtures.

flag lot – a lot shaped like a flag on a flagpole.

flashing – a metallic material that is used in certain areas of the roof and walls to prevent water from seeping into the structure.

flat-fee broker – a broker who for a fixed price will list a property and help the owner sell it.

flip – a real estate term that indicates the buying of real estate expects to resell it immediately at a profit.

float – in construction, a flat hand tool used to smooth the surface of freshly placed concrete after it has been leveled with a darby.

float valve – used to control water levels in tanks.

floating interest rates – fixed FHA loans that are negotiable and float with the market. The seller also has a choice in how many points to contribute toward the borrower's loan.

floating slab – a type of foundation slab constructed by pouring the footing first, then pouring the slab.

flood insurance – insurance coverage for losses to real and personal property resulting from the inundation of normally dry areas from (1) the overflow of inland or tidal waters, (2) the unusual and rapid accumulation or runoff of surface waters, (3) mud slides resulting from accumulations of water on or under the ground, and (4) erosion losses caused by abnormal water runoff.

floodplains – low, flat, periodically flooded lands adjacent to rivers, lake, and oceans that are subject to geomorphic (land shaping) and hydrolic (water flow) processes.

floor joists – framing members that span the distance between the foundation walls and the girder and provide support for the subfloor.

floor truss – a support member constructed in a factory by nailing a number of smaller members (2 3 4s or 2 3 6s) together in a number of triangular patterns to provide maximum strength.

flue – the enclosed passageway in a chimney or attic through which smoke and other gases move upward.

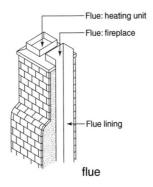

flue

flue collar – the opening on the top, rear, or side of a wood-burning stove to which the stovepipe is connected.

FNMA – See *Federal National Mortgage Association*.

footing – the concrete base below the frost line that supports the foundation of the structure.

for sale by owner (FSBO) – a property that is offered for sale by its owner.

forbear – not to act.

forced warm air system – a type of heating system that contains a fan or blower, a heat source such as gas or oil, a heat exchanger, and filters; works by extracting cool air from indoors and outdoors and passing this cool air through the heat sources.

forcible entry and detainer – a proceeding for restoring the possession of the land to one who has been wrongfully deprived of the possession.

foreclose – to terminate, shut off, or bar a mortgagee's claim to property after default.

foreclosure – the procedure by which a person's property can be taken and sold to satisfy an unpaid debt; effect on leases.

foreclosure sale – the sale of a foreclosed property to satisfy an unpaid debt.

foreign corporation – a corporation organized under the laws of another state or country other than the state or country than that in which it is doing business.

forfeiture of title – the reacquiring of the title on the grounds that the grantee did not use the land for the required purpose.

Form HO-8 – a policy designed for older homes.

formal appraisal – an independently and impartially prepared written statement expressing an opinion of a defined value of an adequately describe property as of a specific date, that is supported by the presentation and analysis of relevant market information.

formal assumption – the property is not conveyed to a new buyer until the new buyer's creditworthiness has been approved by the FHA or its agent.

formal will – See *witnessed will*.

formaldehyde – a colorless, gaseous chemical compound that is generally present at low, variable concentrations in both indoor and outdoor air.

foundation – See *foundation wall*.

foundation wall – generally composed of poured concrete, masonry (concrete) block, or brick; the height of the foundation wall determines whether the structure has a full basement or a crawl space.

Four Corners Doctrine – a doctrine establishing that an instrument is to be examined by reading the whole of it without reference to any one part more than any other.

four unities of a joint tenancy – time, title, interest, and possession.

franchisee – the party who has a franchise.

franchiser – the party giving the franchise.

fraud – an act intended to deceive for the purpose of inducing another to give up something of value.

Freddie Mac – See *Federal Home Loan Mortgage Corporation*.

free and clear title – a title without encumbrances.

freehold estate – an estate in land or other real property of certain duration that may be inherited. It is an estate for life or in fee.

Freon – the most commonly used refrigerant in air conditioners.

friable – the ability of an asbestos-containing product to crumble easily and emit fibers.

frieze board – prevents wind and moisture from penetrating the junction of the soffit and sheathing.

front foot – one linear foot along the street side of a lot; lot appraisal.

frontage – the front side of a lot.

front-end ratio – ratio based on total housing expense.

front-foot basis – a special assessment for the installation of storm drains, curbs, and gutters where the property owner is charged for each foot of his lot that abuts the street being improved.

front-foot value – method of value given to frontage.

fructus industriales – Latin for "fruits of industry"; annual crops planted, cultivated, and harvested through the labor of the land's occupants.

fructus naturales – Latin for "fruits of nature"; plants such as trees and grass that do not require annual planting, and metal obtained from the land.

FSBO – See *for sale by owner*.

FSLIC – See *Federal Savings and Loan Insurance Corporation*.

full covenant and warranty deed – a deed that contains the covenants of seizin, quiet enjoyment, encumbrances, further assurance, and warranty forever. See also *general warranty deed*.

full disclosure – making a full revelation of known information.

full reciprocity – when a state accepts another's real estate license and does not require additional testing.

functional obsolescence – depreciation that results from improvements that are inadequate, overly adequate, or improperly designed for today's needs.

funding fee – a charge by the VA to guarantee a loan.

fungible – freely substitutable.

furring strip – strips applied over a surface to increase thickness or to provide a base for the attachment of other material.

fuse – a device with an internal metal link that melts and opens the circuit, causing electrical power to stop when overheating occurs.

fuse

future advance clause – a clause that secures all items of indebtedness of a mortgagor that shall at any time be owing to the mortgagee.

future interest – interest in land in which the privilege of possession or enjoyment is future and not present; also called a remainder interest.

G

gain – a profit from the sale of an asset; the difference between the adjusted basis and the net selling price.

gain on the sale – the difference between the amount realized and the basis.

gap financing ("swing loan" or "bridge loan") – See *bridge loan*.

gate valve – a type of valve generally used as the main water shutoff valve to the property.

general agency – an agency wherein the agent has the power to bind the principal in a particular trade or business.

general common elements – See *common elements*.

general lien – a lien on all of a person's property.

general partner – a co-owner of a business venture who organizes and operates the partnership, contributes capital, and agrees to accept the full financial liability of the partnership.

general partnerships – See *partnership (general)*.

general plan – See *master plan*.

general warranty deed – a deed in which the grantor warrants or guarantees the title to real property against defects existing before the grantor acquired title or arising during the grantor's ownership. See also *full covenant and warranty deed*.

GFCI – See *ground fault circuit interrupter*.

gift deed – a deed that states "love and affection" as the consideration.

gift letter – a letter stating that the money given is not to be repaid; it is a true gift.

GIM – See *gross income multiplier*.

Ginnie Mae – See *Government National Mortgage Association*.

girder – the main carrying beam, either steel or several wooden members fastened together (usually 2 3 10s, 2 3 12s, or larger), that spans the distance from one side of the foundation to the other.

glazing – the material inside the windowpane.

globe valve – a type of valve that can adjust or stop the flow of water; it is used at points where it is needed infrequently such as in bathrooms.

glue-laminated lumber (glulam) – a structural wood member made by bonding together laminations of dimension lumber.

GNMA – See *Government National Mortgage Association*.

go to bond – a bond issue prepared by government officials that totals the unpaid assessments in the improvement district.

good and chattels – See *chattel*.

good consideration – consideration without monetary value, such as love and affection.

good faith estimate – a form required by the Department of Housing and Urban Development estimating the cost of the loan given in good faith to applicants.

goods and chattels – possessions and personal property.

Government National Mortgage Association (GNMA or "Ginnie Mae") – a government agency that sponsors a mortgage-backed securities program and provides subsidies for residential loans; it is a government sponsored secondary market lending agency.

government rectangular survey method – a system for surveying land that uses latitude and longitude lines as references.

government survey method – a system for surveying land that uses latitude and longitude lines as references.

grade – See *slope*.

grading – the arrangement and preparation of the soil for construction.

Graduate REALTOR® Institute (GRI) – a designation awarded to REALTORS® who complete a prescribed course of real estate study.

graduated payment mortgage – a fixed interest rate loan wherein the monthly payment starts low and then increases, because the initial monthly payments are insufficient to fully amortize the loan.

graduated rental – a lease that provides for agreed-upon rent increases.

grandfather clause – a legal provision that exempts people or businesses from new regulations affecting prior rights or privileges.

grant – the act of conveying ownership.

grant deed – a deed that is somewhat narrower than a warranty deed in terms of covenants and warranties.

grantee – the person named in a deed who acquires ownership.

granting clause – the clause where the grantor states that the intent of the document is to pass ownership to the grantee; part of the words of conveyance.

grantor – the person named in a deed who conveys ownership.

grantor-grantee indexes – alphabetical lists used to locate documents in the public records.

gratuitous agent – a real estate agent that is not compensated for his services.

gravity tank – a large well-water storage tank located above the level of the structure. It differs from other storage tanks because the pressure in a gravity tank is not derived from the amount of water in the tank; rather it is derived from the elevation above the water outlets. See also *well-water storage tank.*

GRI – See *Graduate REALTOR® Institute.*

grid system – state-sponsored survey points to which metes and bounds surveys can be referenced.

GRM – See *gross rent multiplier.*

gross income – the sum of total income received from an operating property before deducting expenses.

gross income multiplier (GIM) – a numerical factor expressing the relationship of gross income to the purchase price of the property.

gross lease – a lease of property under the terms of which the landlord pays all property charges regularly incurred through ownership and the tenant pays a fixed charge for the term of the lease.

gross profit – total income generated before deducting expenses.

gross rent multiplier (GRM) – a number that is multiplied by a property's gross rents to produce an estimate of the property's worth; an economic factor used to estimate a property's market value.

gross sales – total sales.

ground fault circuit interrupter (GFCI) – a device that shuts off a circuit immediately if it senses a short circuit.

ground lease – lease of land only, sometimes secured by the improvements placed on the land by the user.

ground rent – rent paid to occupy a plot of land.

groundwater – water beneath the surface of the earth that can be collected with wells, tunnels, or drainage galleries or that flows naturally to the earth's surface via seeps or springs.

groundwater level – the upper limit of percolating water below the earth's surface.

grout – a mixture of Portland cement, lime, and sand that is mixed with water to fill and seal the spaces between tiles.

guaranty – an assurance given as security that a person's debt will be paid.

guardian's deed – used to convey property of a minor or legally incompetent person.

guide meridian – survey line running north and south that corrects for the earth's curvature.

gypsum board – type of wall panel composed of an inner core of noncombustible gypsum and paper surfacing on the front, back, and edges.

H

habendum clause – the "To have and to hold" clause found in deeds; part of the words of conveyance.

habitability, warranty of – guarantee that premises occupied by a tenant are habitable. The definition of habitability is a fact question and is determined by the jury.

habitable – capable of being lived in.

hacienda – an estate with a large amount of land used for farming and ranching.

handicap access – making public establishments, living facilities, transportation and other places and services accessible to handicapped persons.

handicapped – having a physical or mental impairment which substantially limits one or more major life activities; or having a record of having such an impairment; or being regarded as having such an impairment.

handyman special – property in need of repair.

hardwood – a botanical group of trees that have broad leaves that are shed in the winter. (It does *not* refer to the hardness of the wood.)

hazard insurance – property coverage for such things as fire, wind, storm, and flood damage.

hazardous substance – harmful substance.

hazardous waste – harmful waste material that may cause injury or death.

hazards – See *perils*.

headers – beams that support the ceiling and the roof over the door and window openings.

headroom – the space between the stair and the overhang (or the ceiling inside the structure).

heat exchanger – the area where combustion or the burning of fuel for heat takes place in a furnace or hot water heater.

Hectare Metric system – equivalent to the U.S. measurement of 2.47 acres.

heirs – those designated by law to receive the property of the deceased when there is no will.

heterogeneous – in real estate, it signifies that no two parcels of land are exactly alike because no two parcels can occupy the same position on the globe.

highest and best use – that use of a parcel of land that will produce the greatest current value.

hip roof – a roof consisting of four sloping planes that intersect forming a pyramidal shape.

historic structure – a structure that is well-known or important in history.

HO-2 – See *broad form*.

HO-3 – see *special form*.

HO-4 – See *Tenant's form*.

HO-6 – See *condominium unit owner's form*.

HO-8 – See *Form HO-8*.

HOA – See *homeowners' association*.

holdover tenant – a tenant who stays beyond the lease period and who can be evicted or given a new lease.

holographic will – one that is entirely hand-written and signed by the testator but not witnessed.

home equity line of credit – See *equity mortgage*.

home inspection – an examination of the exterior and interior of residential property including the grounds, the structure, and the mechanical systems to determine structural defects; broken or obsolete components; and damage due to water, wear and tear, and other conditions.

home inspection report – a written itemization and detailed summation of the findings of the home inspector with regard to a subject property.

home inspector – a qualified professional who performs a home inspection.

home loan – a loan made to buy a residential property.

home warranty – a warranty on resale homes that covers mechanical items.

homeowner policy – a combined property and liability policy designed for residential use.

homeowners' association (HOA) – a legal framework so that condominium unit owners can govern themselves; to control, regulate, and maintain the common elements for the overall welfare and benefit of its members. A mini-government by and for condominium owners, it can be organized as a trust or unincorported association, most often it will be organized as a corporation in order to provide the legal protections normally afforded by a corporation to its owners. Additionally, it will be organized as not-for-profit so as to avoid income taxes on money collected from members. A unit purchaser is automatically a member.

home-seller program – a plan whereby FNMA will buy purchase money mortgages from home sellers.

homestead – a legal estate that is a place of residence for a family or a single adult person that is exempt from sale by creditors except under certain specified conditions.

Homestead Act – allows persons to acquire fee title to federal lands.

homestead protection – state laws that protect against the forced sale of a person's home.

homogeneous – essentially alike.

Horizontal Property Act – legislation that permits the creation of condominiums.

house rules – rules regarding day-to-day use of the premises; condominium.

house wrap – exterior insulation material that is nailed over the sheathing.

housing expense ratio (front-end ratio) – loan qualifying ratio based on total housing expenses.

HUD – See *Department of Housing and Urban Development*.

humidifier – a device used to add moisture to the air.

hundred percent commission – an arrangement whereby the salesperson pays for office overhead directly rather than splitting commission income with the broker.

hydronic system – a type of system that heats and cools liquids such as water.

hydrostatic pressure – the push of water against a surface.

hypothecate – to use property to secure a debt without giving up possession of it.

I

iden sonans – a court may be allowed to correct names that sound the same but have been misspelled.

illiquid asset – an asset that may be difficult to sell on short notice.

illiquidity – the possibility that an asset may be very difficult to sell on short notice.

immobility – incapable of being moved, fixed in location; an important physical characteristic of land.

immunity – held by a person or class, against or beyond the course of the law. In libel or slander, an exemption from liability for the speaking or publishing of defamatory words concerning another, based on the fact that the statement was made in the performance of a political, judicial, social, or personal, duty.

implication – type of easement creation.

implied authority – agency authority arising from industry custom, common usage, and conduct of the parties involved rather than expressed agreement.

implied contract – a contract created by the actions of the parties involved.

impound account – See *reserve account*.

improved land – to make land useful and profitable and to increase its value with betterments.

improvement – any form of land development, such as buildings, roads, fences, and pipelines, that generally increase the value of a property.

improvement district – a geographical area that will be assessed for a local improvement.

imputed interest – interest assessed by the IRS on a deferred payment transaction.

imputed notice – constructive notice; notice given by the public records and by visible possession, and the legal presumption that all persons are thereby notified.

in gross – See *easement in gross*.

in perpetuity – continuing forever.

inactive license – when a salesperson's real estate license has been made inactive by the Real Estate Commission.

income approach – a method of valuing property based on the monetary returns that a property can be expected to produce.

income property – rentable, income producing property.

income statement – See *profit and loss statement*

income taxes – taxes paid according to the amount of income received.

incompetent – a person that is not legally capable of entering into a contract.

incorporeal hereditaments – anything, the subject of property, which is inheritable and not tangible or visible.

incorporeal rights – a right without possession in real estate such as an easement.

incurable depreciation – depreciation that cannot be fixed and simply must be lived with.

indemnification – an obligation of the principal in which an agent is entitled to upon suffering a loss through no personal fault, such as when a misrepresentation by the principal to the agent was passed on in good faith to the buyer.

independent appraisal – an appraisal performed by a private individual or company without the order of a lending institution.

independent contractor – one who contracts to do work according to his own methods, tools and equipment, and is responsible to his employer only for the results of that work.

index lease – rent is tied to some economic indicator such as inflation.

index rate – the interest rate to which an adjustable mortgage is tied.

indicated value – the worth of the subject property as shown by recent sales of comparable properties.

inflation – price rises due to the creation of excessive amounts of money by government.

inflation guard – an insurance policy endorsement that automatically increases coverage during the life of a policy.

informal appraisal – an estimate of value.

informal reference – method of identifying a parcel of land by its street address or common name.

ingress – an easement that can be used to go into and out of a property but without the right to park on it.

inheritance – succession of all rights and property to an heir of a deceased person.

inheritance tax – the tax paid on a property inherited by an heir.

in-house sale – a sale made by an agent from the same real estate office that acquired the listing of the sold property.

initial payment – the first payment.

inliquidity – See *illiquidity*.

inner city – a central part of the city that is densely populated.

innocent misrepresentation – wrong information but without the intent to deceive.

inquiry notice – information the law presumes one would have where circumstances, appearances, or rumors warrant further inquiry.

inside lot – a lot with only one side on a street.

installment contract – a method of selling and financing property whereby the seller retains title but the buyer takes possession while making the payments.

installment land contract – an executory contract for sale of real estate, which usually lasts for a term of years.

installment method – the selling of an appreciated property on terms rather than for cash so as to spread out the payment of income taxes on the gain.

installment note – a note that allows payment over an extended period of time.

installment sale benefits – provision in the Internal Revenue Code by which the profit on the sale of one's capital asset can be spread over a series of years.

installment sale contracts – executory contracts for the conveyance of real property.

Institute of Real Estate Management (IREM) – professional designation for property managers.

instrument – a written document capable of being recorded.

insulators – materials that are poor conductors of electricity and are, therefore, placed around wires to prevent electrical shock.

insurable interest – the insured financial interest in a property.

insurable title – a clear title that is capable of being insured.

insurance premium – the amount of money one must pay for insurance coverage.

insurance value – the cost of replacing damaged property.

insured – one who is covered by insurance.

insurer – the insurance company.

inter vivos trust – a trust that is established and takes effect during the lifetime of the trustor.

interest – compensation allowed by law for the use or forbearance or detention of money; deduction.

interest rate cap – the maximum interest rate charge allowed on an adjustable loan.

interim loan (*also called* construction loan) – a loan that is to be replaced by a permanent loan.

interior trim – See *trim.*

interlineations – the act of writing between the lines of an instrument; also what is written between lines.

intermediary – a broker employed to negotiate a transaction between the parties.

intermediate theory – the legal position that a mortgage is a lien until default, at which time title passes to the lender.

Internal Revenue Code of 1986 – body of laws that codify and delineate the levying, collecting, and enforcing of federal tax laws.

internal reversing mechanism – part of a garage door opener, it causes the door to reverse when it hits an obstruction.

interpleader – a legal proceeding to determine which of two parties has the more valid claim against a third party.

interspousal deed – used in some states to transfer real property between spouses.

interstate – transaction and proceedings that take place between and among the several states.

Interstate Land Sales Full Disclosure Act – an act making it unlawful for any land developer (except for certain exempt developers) to sell or lease, by use of the mails or by use of any means of interstate commerce, any land offered as a part of a common promotional plan, unless such land has been registered with the Secretary of the Department of Housing and Urban Development (HUD), and a printed property report is furnished to the purchaser or lessee in advance of the signing of any agreement for sale or lease.

interval ownership – See *time-sharing*.

interval ownership condominiums – ownership of a condominium by exclusive fee title for a period in which the owner is entitled to possession. Unlike timesharing condominiums, the fee title only vests for a period of time and does not change from year to year.

intestate – without a last will and testament.

intestate succession – See *title by descent*.

intrastate – alludes to procedures and transactions which take place entirely within the boundaries of a particular state.

inverse condemnation – a legal action in which an owner demands that a public agency buy his land.

investment – a resource designated to obtain a profit.

investment property – an income producing property.

investment strategy – a plan that balances returns available with risks that must be taken in order to enhance the investor's overall welfare.

investment tax credit – a dollar for dollar credit applicable against taxes due on an investment.

involuntary lien – a lien created by operation of law.

IREM – See *Institute of Real Estate Management*.

irrevocable – unalterable; not changeable.

J

jamb – the vertical member forming the side of a door or window frame.

joint adventure – See *joint venture*.

joint tenancy – a form of property co-ownership that features the right of survivorship.

joint venture – an association of two or more persons or firms in order to carry out a single business project.

jointing – forming control joints in a concrete slab.

jointly and severally liable – enforceable on the makers as a group and upon each maker individually.

joists – wooden framing members used to construct floors and ceilings.

judgment – a court decree to determine a settlement.

judgment lien – a claim against property in favor of the holder of a court-ordered judgment.

judgment roll – a publicly available list of court-ordered judgments.

judicial foreclosure – foreclosure by lawsuit.

judicial sale – a court-ordered sale.

jumbo loan – a very large loan that goes beyond the limits set by the Federal National Mortgage Association (Fannie Mae) and the Federal Home Loan Mortgage Corporation (Freddie Mac).

junction boxes – contain wiring and are used to provide the necessary space for making electrical connections.

junior mortgage – any mortgage on a property that is subordinate to the first mortgage in priority.

jurat – a sworn statement by the person who signed the document that the information contained in the document is true.

jurisdiction – See *original jurisdiction*.

jury – a number of people, selected according to the laws, to inquire of certain matters of fact and declare the truth upon evidence to be laid before them.

just compensation – fair market value of a property as compensation for a "taking."

K

key lot – a lot that adjoins the side or rear property line of a corner lot.

kilowatt – one thousand watts equals one kilowatt.

kilowatt hour – one thousand watts of power consumed in one hour. Ten 100-watt lamps burning for ten hours is one kilowatt hour. Two 500-watt electric heaters operated for two hours is one kilowatt hour.

L

laches – an unreasonable delay in asserting one's rights.

lally columns – round steel columns filled with concrete that support the main carrying beam of the structure, they rest on a base plate, which is the column footing pad.

laminate – a material made by bonding several layers of material.

land – starting at the center of the earth, it passes through the earth's surface, and continues on into space.

land contract – See *installment contract*.

land descriptions – six commonly used methods of describing the location of land: (1) informal reference, (2) metes and bounds, (3) rectangular survey system, (4) recorded plat, (5) assessor's parcel number, and (6) reference to documents other than maps.

land grant – land granted to someone.

land lease – land that has been leased by contract.

land patent – a government document used for conveying public lands in fee to miners and settlers.

land trust – (1) a real estate trust wherein the person who creates the trust (the trustor) is also its beneficiary; (2) a trust created solely for the ownership, operation, and management of real estate interests.

landlord – the owner of an estate in land who has leased the land for a term of years, on a rent reserve, to another person called the tenant.

landmark – a monument or marker that establishes a certain spot, such as the boundary of a property.

land-use control – any legal restriction that controls how a parcel of land may be used.

late charge – a charge for a late payment.

latent defect – a hidden or concealed defect that cannot be discovered by ordinary observation or inspection.

lateral force – a force acting generally in a horizontal direction, such as the wind.

lath – the base material for the application of plaster.

latitude lines – imaginary east-west reference lines that circle the earth.

lawful objective – to be enforceable, a contract cannot call for the breaking of laws.

lead – a toxic metallic element found in soil, water, and paint.

lead-based paint – paint that has a lead component and that is extremely harmful and may be deadly to children.

lease – an agreement that conveys the right to use property for a period of time.

lease with option to buy (lease-option) – allows a tenant to buy the property at present price and terms for a given period of time.

leasehold estate – an estate in land where there is possession but not ownership.

leasehold interest – a tenant's legal interest in a property.

leasehold mortgage – a mortgage loan secured by a tenant's leasehold interest in a property.

lease-option – See *lease with option to buy*.

lease-purchase agreement – an agreement to lease real property and purchase it later.

legacy – See *bequest*.

legal age – See *majority*.

legal consideration – the requirement that consideration be present in a contract.

legal description – a description recognized by law that is sufficient to locate and identify property without oral testimony.

legal notice – See *constructive notice.*

legal rate of interest – rate of interest that follows usury laws.

legal title – one that is complete and perfect in regard to the apparent right of ownership and possession enforceable in a court of law.

legatee – a person who receives personal property under a will.

lender's policy – a title insurance policy designed to protect a lender.

lessee – See *tenant.*

lessee's interest – the interest a tenant has in a property.

lessor – See *landlord.*

lessor's interest – the interest a landlord has in a property.

letter of credit – a bank letter of obligation.

letter of intent – a document that expresses mutual intent but without liability or obligation.

leverage – the impact that borrowed funds have on an investment return.

liability – anything owed to an individual, a bank, or a business.

LIBOR – See *London Interbank Offered Rate.*

license – a personal privilege to use land on a nonexclusive basis.

license reciprocity – when one state honors another's real estate license.

license revocation – to recall and make void a license.

license suspension – to temporarily make a license ineffective.

license, real estate. – See *real estate license*; *real estate regulation*.

licensee – one who holds a license from a government or other agency which permits a person to pursue some occupation according to certain standards, such as real estate sales.

lien – a hold or charge on a property for the payment of some debt, obligation, or duty owed to lien holder.

lien release – the releasing of a lien due to payment of the loan.

lien theory – the legal position that a mortgage creates a charge against property rather than conveying it to the lender.

lienee – the party subject to a lien.

lienholder – See *lienor*.

lienor – the party holding a lien.

life estate – an estate whose duration is limited to the life of the party holding it or some other person.

life interest – interest in property for the duration of life.

life tenant – one who possesses a life estate.

lifetime cap – the maximum interest rate adjustment permitted over the life of a loan.

lift handle – affixed to a garage overhead door (or a pull rope attached to the bottom bracket in the lower corner of the door) and used with a door that is opened and closed manually.

light – a layer of a glass window; windows may have one or more.

like-kind property – property equal in quality or usage.

limestone – a sedimentary rock consisting of calcium and magnesium.

limited appraisal – the act or process of estimating value performed under and resulting from invoking the Departure Provision.

limited common elements – those common elements that are agreed upon by all of the co-owners to be reserved for the use of a certain number of apartments to the exclusion of the other apartments, such as special corridors, stairways, and elevators, sanitary services common to the apartments of a particular floor, etc.

limited liability company – a form of business organization, combining the most favorable attributes of a partnership and a corporation, and consisting of members or managers that is governed by its by-laws.

limited liability partnership – a form of ownership that attempts to limit the liability of general partners from the misconduct of other general partners.

limited partner – a partner who provides capital but does not take personal financial liability nor participate in management.

limited partnership – a combination of general partners who, under the provisions of the Uniform Limited Partnership Act, operate the partnership and take personal financial liability and limited partners who provide the bulk of the capital.

limited partnership agreement – the agreement that sets forth the details and agreements of the general and limited partners to a limited partnership agreement.

line of credit – the maximum amount of credit a bank will lend a borrower.

link – in land measurements, a link equals 7.9 inches.

lintel – a beam spanning an opening in a wall.

liquid asset – an asset that can be converted to cash on short notice.

liquidated damages – an amount of money specified in a contract as compensation to be paid if the contract is not satisfactorily completed.

liquidity – a resource that is readily convertible into cash.

lis pendens – a public notice indicating that a lawsuit has been filed because title to real estate is in controversy.

listing – a contract wherein a broker is employed to find a buyer or tenant and perform other real estate brokerage services.

listing agent – the real estate agent that procured the listing agreement.

listing agreement – a contract authorizing a broker to sell, buy, or lease real property on behalf of another, and giving the agent the right to collect a commission if the property is sold through his efforts.

littoral right – the lawful claim of a landowner to use and enjoy the water of a lake or sea bordering the land.

live load – nonpermanent moving or movable external loads on a structure, such as furniture or snow.

load – the electric power used by devices connected to an electrical system. Loads can be figured in amperes, volt-amperes, kilovolt-amperes, or kilowatts. Loads can be intermittent, continuous intermittent, periodic, short-time, or varying.

load-bearing – carrying an imposed load.

loan – money that is lent to a borrower whom is obligated to repay it.

loan application – an application made to obtain a loan.

loan balance table – shows the balance remaining to be paid on an amortized loan.

loan broker – the middleman between the lender and the applicant.

loan brokerage fees – fees paid to a mortgage broker for locating and obtaining funds for a borrower.

loan closing – the closing, or final settlement, of a loan or refinancing of a loan.

loan commitment letter – a written agreement that a lender will make a loan.

loan constant – the outstanding debt expressed as percentage of the loan amount.

loan escrow – an escrow account opened for the purpose of repaying a loan.

loan origination fee – the amount a lender charges for processing a mortgage loan.

loan package – all the necessary loan forms and requirements to obtain a loan.

loan points – a charge, expressed in percentage points, to obtain a loan.

loan policy – the lender's requirements to obtain a loan.

loan servicing – the task of collecting monthly payments and handling insurance and tax impounds, delinquencies, early payoffs, and mortgage leases.

loan value – value set on a property for the purpose of making a loan.

loan-to-value ratio – a percentage reflecting what a lender will lend divided by the market value of the property.

location preference – See *situs*.

lockbox – a strongbox kept on or near the premises for the keys to the property for sale. Real estate agents use lockboxes to allow other agents convenient access to the listed property.

London Interbank Offered Rate (LIBOR) – an international money market interest rate; an international version of the prime rate.

longitude lines – imaginary north-south reference lines that circle the earth.

long-term capital gain – See *capital gain*.

long-term lease – a lease for one year or longer.

long-term loan – real estate financing available for repayment for more than 5 to 10 years or a longer period of time.

loose money – means that lenders have adequate funds to loan and are actively seeking borrowers.

lot, block, tract system – See *recorded plat*.

louver – a unit composed of sloping vanes used to restrict the entry of rain into openings in exterior walls yet permit the flow of air through the opening.

love and affection – a term used as the consideration given by a loved one in a contract.

loyalty to principal – a requirement that an agent place his principal's interest above his or her own.

M

M and M lien – See *mechanics* and *materialmen lien*.

MAI – member, American Institute of Real Estate Appraisers.

main soil stack – a drainage pipe that connects to the house drain where waste leaves the system.

main vent stack – the top of the main soil stack that connects to all of the home's toilets.

maintenance – the upkeep of a property.

maintenance fees – See *association dues*.

majority – the minimum age required for legal competency (in most states 18 years).

maker – the person who signs a promissory note. See also *obligor*.

management company – a company that advises the condominium board and takes care of day-to-day tasks.

management contract – a contract detailing responsibilities of the owner and the manager of a property.

manufactured housing – the 1976 Department of Housing and Urban Development imposed replacement of "mobile home."

mapping requirements – regulations a subdivider must meet before selling lots.

marble – a metamorphic rock formed largely of calcite, dolomite, or dense limestone.

margin – the amount added to the index rate that reflects the lender's cost of doing business.

marginal land – land that barely repays the cost of production.

marginal release – a notation on the recorded mortgage that shows the book and page location of the mortgage release.

market comparison approach – a method of valuing a property based on the prices of recent sales of similar properties.

market data approach – See *market comparison approach*.

market value – the cash price that a willing buyer and a willing seller would agree upon, given reasonable exposure of the property to the marketplace, full information as to the potential uses of the property, and no undue compulsion to act.

marketable title – title that is free from reasonable doubt as to who is the owner.

Marketable Title Act – state law aimed at cutting off rights and interest in land that has been inactive for long periods.

master deed – the deed, lease, or declaration establishing a parcel of land as a condominium subdivision.

master lease – See *master deed*.

master limited partnership (MLP) – limited partnerships that can be traded on a stock exchange nearly as easily as corporate stock.

master plan – a comprehensive guide describing the long-term land use and management goals for the physical growth of a community.

material fact – an important fact considered by the buyer in his decision to purchase a property.

materialman – one who has furnished materials or labor for an improvement.

materialman lien – a lien placed on a property for work and/or materials until the debt is repaid.

matured interest – interest that is due and payable.

maturity (*also called* the maturity date) – the end of the life of a loan.

MBS – See *mortgage-backed securities*.

mechanics and materialmen – individuals or companies who supply labor, services, or materials for the construction of improvements on real estate.

mechanics and materialmen lien – a claim or hold placed against property by unpaid workers or materials suppliers.

mediation – an alternative to settle problems that may arise in a real estate transaction instead of going to court.

mediator – an impartial person that assists opposing parties in settling problems.

medical payments coverage – a homeowner's policy that covers the cost of treating minor injuries.

meeting of the minds (*also called* mutual agreement) – means that there must be agreement to the provisions of a contract by all parties involved.

menace – threat of violence to obtain a contract.

merchantable title – See *marketable title*.

meridian – imaginary lines running north and south, used as references in mapping land.

metal lath – available in a variety of styles and resembling a mesh or honeycomb pattern, the lath supports the plaster that hardens around it.

metes and bounds – a detailed method of land description that identifies a parcel by specifying its shape and boundaries.

metropolitan area – a large city and its surrounding communities.

MGIC – See *Mortgage Guarantee Insurance Corporation*.

middleman – a person who brings two or more parties together but does not conduct negotiations.

mile – 5,280 feet or 1,760 yards.

mill rate – property tax rate expressed in tenths of a cent per dollar of assessed valuation.

mineral interests – an interest in the minerals in land, including the right to take minerals or the right to receive a royalty on those minerals.

minor – a person under the age of legal competence (in most states, under 18 years).

misrepresentation – See *innocent misrepresentation*.

mistake – refers to ambiguity in contract negotiations and mistake of material fact.

mitigation of damages – the lessening of the intensity of damages.

MLP – See *master limited partnership*.

MLS – See *multiple listing service*.

modification – the influence on land use and value resulting from improvements made by man to surrounding parcels.

monetary base – the legal reserves of banks at the Federal Reserve.

monetize the debt – the creation of money by the Federal Reserve to purchase Treasury securities.

money damages – compensation paid in lieu of contract performance.

monolithic slab – a type of foundation slab where the footing and slab are poured at the same time.

monopoly – a private interest vested in one or more persons or companies consisting of the exclusive right to carry on a particular business or trade.

month-to-month lease – a lease that renews itself each month.

monument – an iron pipe, stone, tree, or other fixed point used in making a survey.

moratorium – the legal period of delay for meeting a financial obligation.

mortar – a plastic mixture of cementitious materials, water, and a fine aggregate.

mortgage – a document that makes property secure for the repayment of a debt.

mortgage banker – a person who makes mortgage loans and then sells them to investors.

mortgage broker – a person who brings borrowers and lenders together, a loan broker.

mortgage company – a firm that makes mortgage loans and then sells them to investors.

Mortgage Guarantee Insurance Corporation (MGIC) – a private mortgage insurer that provides numerous products and services to mortgage lenders' ability to meet the home loan needs.

mortgage insurance – insures lenders against nonrepayment of loans.

mortgage lien – a pledge of property by its owner to secure the repayment of a debt.

mortgage pool – a common fund of mortgage loans in which one can invest.

mortgage reduction – when an investor uses a portion of a property's rental income to reduce the balance owing on the mortgage.

mortgage servicing – the service right and fee the secondary lender gives to the primary lender for maintaining loans.

mortgage-backed securities (MBS) – certificates that pass through principal and interest payments to investors.

mortgagee – the party receiving the mortgage, the lender.

mortgagee's information letter – a document prepared by a lender that shows the balance due on an existing loan.

mortgagee's policy – title insurance policy designed to protect a lender.

mortgagee-mortgagor indexes – alphabetical lists used to locate mortgages in the public records.

mortgage-equity tables – tables available from bookstores used to find a value for property.

mortgagor – the party giving the mortgage, the borrower.

mortgagor-mortgagee indexes – alphabetical lists used to locate mortgages in the public records.

Mother Hubbard clause – See *additional property clause*.

mullion – horizontal or vertical members between adjacent window or door units.

multiple listing – an agreement among brokers who belong to the Multiple Listing Service that all listings will be placed on a mutually available list, that all brokers may sell any property on the list, and that the commission will be split in a predetermined fashion.

multiple listing service (MLS) – organization of member brokers agreeing to share listing information and share commissions. See also *multiple listing*.

municipal bond – source of home loans that in turn is financed by the sale of municipal bonds.

muntins – dividers that separate a window sash into smaller windows; may be a fake inset.

mutual agreement (*also called* mutual consent) – an agreement to the provisions of the contract by all parties involved.

mutual consent – See *mutual agreement*.

mutual rescission – voluntary cancellation of a contract by all parties involved.

N

naked title – title that lacks the usual rights and privileges of ownership.

NAR – See *National Association of REALTORS®*

narrative report – is written in paragraph form and reflects the inspector's observation and opinion of the condition of a subject property.

narrative report with checklist or rating system – a narrative report combined with a checklist or rating system report that more fully explains the inspector's observations of the subject property.

National Association of Real Estate Brokers (NAREB) – See *realtist*.

National Association of REALTORS® (NAR) – the dominant real estate industry trade association in the United States.

National Electric Code – national standard for electrical installation and service.

natural person – a live person, not a corporation.

negative amortization – occurs when the interest rate rises to the point that the monthly loan payment is insufficient to pay the interest due and the excess is added to the balance owed, thereby creating an increasing loan balance rather than an amortizing or decreasing loan balance.

negative cash flow – a condition wherein the case paid out exceeds the cash received.

negative leverage – occurs when borrowed funds cost more than they produce.

negotiable instrument – an instrument signed by a maker or drawer, containing an unconditional promise to pay a certain sum of money, which can be passed freely from one person to another. This is often reflected in a promissory note or bank draft.

neighborhood shopping center – several buildings grouped together with 15 or more retail bays; easily accessible to the nearby neighborhood.

net ground lease – a lease for the land where the tenant builds the improvements, and pays for the maintenance, insurance, and taxes.

net income – the total income minus costs and expenses.

net income multiplier – the multiple of net income in relation to all of the fixed expenses.

net lease – a commercial lease wherein the tenant pays a base rent plus maintenance, property taxes, and insurance.

net listing – a listing wherein the commission is the difference between the selling price and a minimum price set by the seller.

net loss – the loss after all charges and deductions.

net operating income (NOI) – gross income less operating expenses, vacancies, and collecting losses.

net proceeds – the total profits derived from a sale minus the expenses.

net rental – rent gained as clear profit.

net spendable – the number of dollars remaining each year after collecting rents and paying operating expenses and mortgage payments.

net worth – total assets minus total debts.

neutral bus bar – a conductor on the main panel board that is the connection for the neutral and ground wires.

new for old – policy pays replacement cost.

NOI – See *net operating income*.

non-assumption clause – a clause in a note or mortgage that gives the lender the right to call the entire loan balance due if the property is sold or otherwise conveyed (also call an alienation clause or a due on-sale clause).

nonbearing wall – a wall that does not carry a load.

non-catalytic stove – a wood-burning stove that maximizes combustion efficiency by providing a secondary combustion air system.

nonconforming loan – a loan that does not follow uniform documentation and qualification parameters set by Fannie Mae and Freddie Mac.

nonconforming use – an improvement that is inconsistent with current land use zoning regulations.

nonexclusive listing – a listing where more than one person can sell the property.

nonfreehold estate – a leasehold estate.

nonfungible – not substitutable.

nonhomogeneity – no two parcels of land are alike (also called heterogeneity).

nonjudicial foreclosure – foreclosure is conducted by the lender.

nonperforming loan – a loan wherein the borrower is behind in his payments.

nonpotable water – wastewater or recycled water used in plumbing fixtures that is not safe for consumption.

nonprofit corporation – a corporation that is established to not make a profit.

nonrecourse financing – the investor is not personally obligated to repay.

nonresident license – out-of-state broker's license.

notary public – an authority appointed by the Secretary of State to take acknowledgment or proofs of written instruments, protest instruments permitted by law to be protested, administer oaths, and take depositions, as is now or may hereafter be conferred by law upon county clerks.

note – See *promissory note.*

notice of consent – allows the secretary of state to receive legal summonses for non-residents.

notice of default – public notice that a borrower is in default.

notice of lis pendens – notice of a pending lawsuit.

notice of revocation – the legal notice revoking consent to use land.

novation – the substitution of a new contract or new party for an old one.

nuisance law – a law of common law origin, similar in all states, that provides that no one shall unreasonably interfere with an individual's enjoyment of his or her property. Such unreasonable interferences legally constitutes a nuisance.

null and void – not legally valid or enforceable.

nuncupative will – an oral will declared or dictated by the testator in his or her last sickness before a sufficient number of witnesses that may pass on only personal property.

O

oakum – a caulking material made from hemp fibers treated with tar.

obedience – See *faithful performance*.

obligee – the person to whom a debt or obligation is owed.

obligor – the person responsible for paying a debt or obligation.

obsolescence – See *economic obsolescence*.

occupancy permit – a permit indicating that a property is habitable.

offer – a proposal to make a contract.

offer and acceptance – the requirement of the offeror to make an offer to the offeree.

offeree – the party who receives an offer.

offeror – the party who makes an offer.

Office of Thrift Supervision (OTS) – organization that authorizes institutions to make the type of adjustable mortgage loan that will most likely be encountered in today's loan marketplace.

offset statement – a statement by an owner or lienholder as to the balance due on existing lien.

off-site management – refers to those property management functions that can be performed away from the premises being managed. See also *property manager*.

ohm – unit of measurement for resistance to the flow of electricity; unit of electrical resistance of a conductor.

old for old – a policy that pays only the depreciated cost.

on-site management – refers to those property management functions that must be performed on the premises being managed. See also *property manager*.

open agency listing – an authorization given by a property owner to a real estate agent wherein the agent is given the nonexclusive right to secure a purchaser.

open house – the showing of a house for promotional purposes.

open listing – a listing that gives a broker a nonexclusive right to find a buyer.

open space – See *public open space*.

open-end mortgage – a mortgage allowing for future revisions secured by the same mortgage.

open-end mortgage – a mortgage that allows the mortgagor to borrow additional funds and extend the amount of the loan without changing the terms of the mortgage.

operating expense – expenditure necessary to operate a property and maintain the production of income.

operating expense ratio – total operating expenses divided by effective gross income.

operating income – See *cash flow*.

opinion of title – an attorney's opinion as to the status of the title.

option – a right, for a given period of time, to buy, sell, or lease property at specified price and terms.

option clause – gives the right at some future time to purchase or lease a property at a predetermined price.

optionee – the party receiving the option.

optionor – the party giving the option.

oral contract – See *express contract*.

oral will – See *nuncupative will*.

ordinance – a city or county legislature enactment, such as a zoning law.

ordinary income – income earned in a usual and customary manner.

original basis – the original cost of an asset.

original contractor – a contractor who has the direct contractual relationship with the owner of the property or his agent.

original jurisdiction – having jurisdiction to hear the case for the first time, before it is tried in any other court, or appealed.

origination fee – See *loan origination fee*.

ostensible agency – agency created by the principal when the principal leads third parties to believe an unaware person is his agent.

ostensible authority – results when a principal gives a third party reason to believe that another person is the agent even though that person is unaware of the appointment.

OTS – See *Office of Thrift Supervision*.

outlet – a point on a wiring system where current is taken to supply equipment.

outside of escrow – See *outside of the closing*.

outside of the closing – a party to the closing pays someone directly and not through the closing (also called *outside of escrow*).

overage – an excess amount of money in escrow.

overall rate – a mortgage-equity factor used to appraise income-producing property.

overcurrent protection device – responds quickly to ground faults; includes the main disconnect, circuit breakers, and fuses.

overencumbered property – occurs when the market value of a property is exceeded by the loans against it.

OWC – See *owner will carry*.

owner of record – the owner named in the official public records.

owner will carry (OWC) – the note amount the seller will carry as a junior mortgage.

owner's policy – a title insurance policy designed to protect the fee owner.

owners' association – an administrative association composed of each unit owner in a condominium.

ownership – a person's legal right of possession.

ownership –the right to process and use property to the exclusion of all others.

P

P&L – See *profit and loss statement*.

package mortgage – a mortgage secured by a combination of real and personal property.

package trust deed – See *package mortgage*.

panic peddling – See *blockbusting*.

paper – See *"taking back paper."*

par – the lender's wholesale price without premiums or discounts.

par value – an equality in value.

parapet – the top of an exterior wall that extends above the line of the roof.

parcel – a piece of land.

parol evidence rule – permits oral evidence to augment a written contract in certain cases.

partial eviction – See *constructive eviction*.

partial reciprocity – when a state gives credit to the licensees of another state for experience, education, and examination.

partial reconveyance – See *partial release*.

partial release – a release of a portion of a property from a mortgage.

partial release fees – fees paid to the lender for a partial release of property, which is secured by a note.

partial taking – occurs during eminent domain when only a portion of the property is taken.

partially amortized loan – a loan that begins with amortized payments but ends with a balloon payment.

participating broker – also known as the co-broker, other broker, selling broker; the broker that procures the buyer.

participation certificate (PC) – a secondary mortgage market instrument whereby an investor can purchase an undivided interest in a pool of mortgages.

participation clause – See *escalation clause*.

participation loan – one that requires interest plus a percentage of the profits.

partition – to divide jointly held property into distinct portions so that each co-owner may hold his or her proportionate share in severalty.

partition action – See *partition*.

partner (general) – a member of a partnership who has united with others to form a partnership business.

partnership (general) – a form of co-owner-ship for business purposes wherein all partners have a voice in its management and unlimited liability for its debts.

party (parties) – a legal term that refers to a person or a group involved in a legal pro-ceeding.

party wall easement – a fence or wall erected along a property line for the mutual benefit of both owners.

passive income – income derived solely from an investment of money in an enterprise that is managed by another, such as a limited partnership.

passive income – income gained from a passive activity such as rental income.

passive investor – an investor who can deduct losses only against income from other passive investments.

passive loss – a loss from a passive activity.

passive solar heating – solar systems that use natural means to store solar energy.

pass-through – a process by which the benefits are passed on.

pass-through securities – certificates that pass mortgage principal and interest payments on to investors.

patent – original land grant from the sovereign power.

patio – a structure that generally abuts the property and is accessed from the house through a simple doorway, most commonly sliding glass doors or French doors. Its material consists of poured concrete, brick, slate, or stones laid in a concrete base.

paver – a type of tile that is either glazed or unglazed and is weather resistant. These tiles are primarily used in commercial applications.

payee – See *obligee*.

payment cap – a limit on how much a borrower's payments can increase.

PC – See *participation certificate*.

penalty – a punishment imposed for a violation of a law or a rule.

percentage lease – lease on property, the rental for which is based on the tenant's sales; usually a percentage of gross receipts from the business with a provision for a minimum rental.

percolating water – underground water not confined to a defined underground waterway.

percolation rate – the speed at which standing water is absorbed by the soil.

perfecting the lien – the filing of a lien statement within the required time limit.

performance – principal is expected to do whatever he reasonably can to accomplish the purpose of the agency, such as referring inquires by prospective buyers to the broker.

perils – hazards or risks.

periodic estate – a tenancy that provides for continuing automatic renewal until canceled, such as a month-to-month rental.

periodic tenancy – See *periodic estate*.

perpetual care fund – a fund provided for by statute for maintaining cemeteries, which requires the creation of a fund that never ceases and is continuous for the maintenance of the cemetery or graveyard.

perpetuity – See *rule against perpetuities*.

personal liability – See *public liability*.

personal property – a right or interest in things of a temporary or movable nature, associated with a person or belongings to an individual; anything not classed as real property.

personal representative – a person named to settle an estate.

personalty – See *personal property*.

phase 1 audit – the first phase of an environmental assessment.

photoelectric eye – sensor mounted five to six inches off the floor on both sides of a garage door.

physical deterioration – deterioration from wear and tear and the action of nature.

pier – a column designed to support a load.

piggyback loan – a combination of two loans in one mortgage.

pilaster –a vertical projection from a masonry or concrete wall providing increased stiffening.

pile – a wood, steel, or concrete column usually driven into the soil to be used to carry a vertical load.

pitch – the slope of the roof.

PITI payment – a loan payment that combines principal, interest, taxes, and insurance.

PITI – See *PITI payment*.

plaintiff – the person who sues.

plan – (1) a line drawing (by floor) representing the horizontal geometrical section of the walls of a building. The section (a horizontal plane) is taken at an elevation to include the relative positions of the walls, partitions, windows, doors, chimneys, columns, pilasters, etc. (2) a plan can be thought of as cutting a horizontal section through a building at an eye level elevation.

planned unit development (PUD) – individually owned lots and houses with community ownership of common areas.

plaster – a cementitious material, usually a mixture of portland cement, lime or gypsum, sand, and water. Used to finish interior walls and ceilings.

plat – a recorded subdivision map that shows the lots, their sizes, and where they are situated in the subdivision.

plat map – See *recorded plat*.

plate – See *sole plate*.

platform framing – the structure's framing rests on a subfloor platform; the most common type of framing used in residential construction.

pledging – giving up possession of property while it serves as collateral for a debt.

plenum – a large metal conduit box in the form of a duct located inside the heating system where hot air builds up pressure and is then forced out to room heating elements.

plottage value – the result of combining two or more parcels of land so that the one large parcel has more value than the sum of the individual parcels.

plumb – a position or measurement that is truly and exactly vertical, 90 degrees from a level surface.

plumbing fixture – an appliance requiring a water supply and drainage system.

ply – one of a number of layers in a layered construction.

plywood – a glued wood panel made up of thin layers of wood veneer with the grain of adjacent layers at right angles to each other or of outer veneers glued to a core of solid wood or reconstituted wood.

PMI – See *private mortgage insurance*.

point – one percent of the loan mount paid to the lender or the lender's agent at the time the loan is made.

point of beginning or point of commence-ment – the starting place at one corner of a parcel of land in a metes and bounds survey.

police power – the right of government, either federal, state, or local, to enact laws and enforce them for the order, safety, health, morals, and general welfare of the public.

portfolio loan – a loan that a lender keeps in its portfolio instead of selling it.

positive cash flow – a condition wherein cash received exceeds cash paid out.

positive leverage – occurs when the benefits of borrowing exceed the costs of borrowing.

possession date – the day on which the buyer can move in.

post and lintel – See *post and beam framing*.

post-and-beam framing – framing members are much larger than ordinary studs and may be four or six inches square; the larger posts are placed several feet apart instead of 16 or 24 inches on center.

potable water – water that is safe for drinking.

powderpost beetle – a type of insect that eats wood.

power of attorney – a written authorization to another to act on one's behalf.

power of sale – allows a mortgagee to conduct a foreclosure sale without first going to court.

pre-inspection agreement – a contract that protects both the home inspector and the client. It explains, in general terms, the scope of the inspection (what is included and what is not), the cost, and the procedures to address any dispute that may arise.

prenuptial agreement – agreement made between a man and woman prior to their marriage concerning the designation of separate and community property.

prepaid interest – the interest paid by the borrower for the time period between the closing and the first payment.

prepaid items – items paid in advance, such as taxes and insurance that are paid monthly with the principal and interest payment.

prepayment penalty – a fee charged by a lender for permitting a borrower to repay a loan early.

prepayment privilege – allows the borrower to repay early without penalty.

prescription (easement by) – a mode of acquiring the right to use property by long continued enjoyment, at least for 10 years.

pressure regulator valve (PRV) – also called a pressure-reducing valve; a type of valve that limits the water pressure, it reduces and automatically maintains the pressure of water within predetermined parameters.

pressure tank – a well-water storage tank that, filled with water, compresses the air inside the tank. As more water is added, the pressure inside the tank increases because the air takes up less volume. As the water is used, the compressed air pushes the water out of the tank under pressure. As the water level drops in the tank, the volume that the air occupies grows and the pressure it exerts decreases. See also *well-water storage tank*.

prevailing rate – the predominant interest rate.

price fixing – a conspiracy by two or more participants to fix prices, goods, or services, effectively eliminating competition in the marketplace.

prima facie – at first view; something that is evident when viewed.

primary industry – See *base industry*.

primary market – a market in which lenders originate loans and make funds available to borrowers.

primary mortgage market – See *primary market*.

prime contractor – See *original contractor*.

prime rate – the minimum interest rates charged to the best-rated customers.

primogeniture – the exclusive right possessed by the eldest son of a family to succeed to the estate of his ancestor, exclusive of the rights of the other sons or children.

principal – a person who authorizes another to act for him; the balance owing on a loan; principal's obligations to agent.

principal broker – the broker in charge of a real estate office.

principal meridian – a longitude line selected as a reference in the rectangular survey system.

principals only – an arrangement in which the owner is contacted by person(s) who want to buy and not by agents.

principle of anticipation – what a person will pay for a property depends on the expected benefits from the property in the future.

principle of change – real property uses are always in a state of change.

principle of competition – where substantial profits are being made, competition will be encouraged.

principle of conformity – the maximum value is realized when there is a reasonable degree of homogeneity in the neighborhood.

principle of contribution – See *principle of diminishing marginal returns.*

principle of diminishing marginal returns – the relationship between added cost and the value it returns.

principle of substitution – the maximum value of a property tends to be set by the cost of purchasing an equally desirable substitute property.

principle of supply and demand – the ability of people to pay for land coupled with the relative scarcity of land.

principles of value – anticipation, change, competition, conformity, diminishing marginal returns, highest and best use, substitution, supply and demand.

prior appropriation – See *doctrine of prior appropriation.*

private mortgage insurance (PMI) – insures lenders against foreclosure loss.

privilege – an exceptional or extraordinary power of exemption, a right, power, franchise, or immunity held by a person or class, against or beyond the course of the law. In libel or slander, an exemption from liability for the speaking or publishing of defamatory words concerning another, based on the fact that the statement was made in the performance of a political, judicial, social, or personal, duty.

privity of contract – the connection or relationship that exists between two or more contracting parties.

pro forma statement – a projected annual operating statement that shows expected income, operating expenses, and net operating income.

probate court – a court of law with the authority to verify the legality of a will and carry out its instructions.

probate sale – the sale of the estate of a deceased person.

proceeds of sale – the total amount received from a sale.

procuring cause – the claim made by a buyer's real estate agent that the foundation for negotiation and the consummation of the sale would not have taken place without his or her efforts.

professional liability insurance – covers individuals and business organizations for claims made by third parties.

profit – a gain from employing capital in a transaction.

profit a prendre – See *easement*.

profit and loss statement (P&L) – a statement showing the gains and losses of a business.

profitability – See *break even points*, *capital gain*.

project – See *condominium project*.

projected gross – See *scheduled gross*.

promissory note – a written promise or engagement to repay a debt.

promulgated forms – mandatory real estate forms created and mandated by state agencies to regulate real estate practices.

property – owner's interest and rights in his or her property to the exclusion of all others; the land and anything permanently attached, such as buildings, fences, and fixtures.

property damage – effect on contracts.

property disclosure statement – government-required information that must be given to purchasers in subdivisions.

property manager – one who supervises every aspect of a property's operation and performs tasks such as renting, tenant relations, building repair and maintenance, accounting, advertising, and supervision of personnel and tradespeople. See also *certified property manager (CPM)*.

property report – government-required information that must be given to purchasers in subdivisions.

property tax lien – the right of government to collect taxes from property owners.

property taxes – taxes levied against land. They are the largest, single source of income in America for local government programs and services. Schools, fire and police departments, local welfare programs, public libraries, street maintenance, parks, and public hospital facilities are mainly supported by property taxes. Some state governments also obtain a portion of their revenues from this source.

proprietary lease – a lease issued by a cooperative corporation to its shareholders.

prorating – the division of ongoing expenses and income items between the buyer and the seller.

prospect – a potential real estate client.

prospectus – a disclosure statement that describes an investment opportunity.

protected class – a class of people that by law are protected from discrimination.

PRV – See *pressure regulator valve*.

public auction – the process of obtaining the best possible price for the property by inviting competitive bidding and conducting the sale in full view of the public.

public grant – transfer of land by a government body to a private individual.

public housing – government subsidized housing for the financially disadvantaged.

public improvement – one that benefits the public at large and is financed through general property taxes.

public land – land owned by the government.

public liability – the financial responsibility one has toward others.

public open space – land that is not expressly developed for residential, commercial, industrial, or institutional use. It can be owned by private individuals or by the public (government ownership) and it can include agricultural and forest land, undeveloped shorelines, public parks, and lakes and bays.

public recorder's office – a government-operated facility wherein documents are entered in the public records.

public trustee – a publicly appointed official who acts as a trustee in some states.

PUD – See *planned unit development*.

puffing – nonfactual or extravagant statements a reasonable person would recognize as such.

punitive damages – damages awarded by a court for mental suffering and anguish.

pur autre vie – a life estate created for the life of another.

purchase agreement – a written contract to purchase real estate.

purchase agreement – an offer to purchase that becomes a binding contract when accepted by the owner of a property.

purchase contract – See *binder*.

purchase money mortgage – a loan used to purchase the real property that serves as its collateral.

Q

quadrangle – a 24-by-24-mile area created by the guide meridians and correction lines in the rectangular survey system.

quadruplex – a building consisting of four units.

qualified buyer – a buyer that has gone through the process of being qualified for a loan.

qualified fee estate – a fee simple estate subject to certain limitations imposed by its grantor (grantor).

qualified intermediary – the third-party escrow agent used in tax-deferred exchange.

quantity survey method – the totaling of all the component parts in the construction plus adding labor costs to arrive at an exact cost of the total project.

quantum meruit – an action found in common law, founded on the implied promise on the part of the defendant to pay the plaintiff as much as he reasonably deserved to have for his labor.

quarry tile – a type of clay tile that does not have a glaze and the surface is sometimes roughened to make the tile slip resistant.

quarter-section – 160 acres.

quasi-contractual recovery – an obligation similar in character to that of a contract, which arises not from an express agreement of the parties, but rather from one that is implied by the court.

quasi-judicial – See *quasi-contractual recovery*.

quiet enjoyment – the right of possession and use of property without undue disturbance by others.

quiet title suit – court-ordered hearings held to determine land ownership.

quitclaim deed – a legal instrument used to convey whatever title the grantor has; it contains no covenants, warranties, or implications of the grantor's ownership.

quorum – the minimum number of members needed at any official meeting in order to conduct business (usually more than half).

R

raceway – used to support, enclose, and protect electrical wires.

racial steering – See *steering*.

radiant heat – heat transferred by radiation.

radon – a colorless, odorless, tasteless, radioactive gas that is present in the environment as a byproduct of the natural decay of uranium in the earth.

rafters – the long wooden framing members that are fastened to the ends of the ceiling joists and form the gables of the roof.

rails – top and bottom pieces of the window sash.

rake – the board along the sloping edge of a gable.

RAM – See *reverse annuity mortgage*.

range lines – a six-mile-wide column of land running north-south in the rectangular survey system.

rate index – the index that adjusts interest rates.

rate of return – the return percentage of an investment.

ratification – an action that takes place after the fact.

rating system report – uses a numerical evaluation on a scale, for example 1-5, to define the condition of each property component.

raw land – undeveloped land.

ready, willing, and able buyer – a buyer who is ready to buy at price and terms acceptable to the owner.

real – inflation-adjusted.

real chattel – an interest in real estate that is personal property, such as leasehold estate.

real estate – any land and its improvements in a physical sense, as well as the rights to own or use both.

real estate broker – a person licensed to act independently in conducting a real estate brokerage business.

real estate commission – a state board that advises and sets policies regarding real estate licenses and transaction procedures; the fee paid to a broker.

real estate commissioner – a person appointed by the governor to implement and carry out laws enacted by the legislature that pertain to real estate.

real estate department – a state office responsible for such matters as license examinations, license issuance, and compliance with state license and subdivision laws.

real estate division – See *real estate department*.

Real Estate Investment Trust (REIT) – a method of pooling investor money by using the trust form of ownership and featuring single taxation of profits. It usually involves a very large amount of investors.

real estate license – granted to real estate salespersons, brokers, and lenders, authorizing them to perform real estate services for persons within their states.

real estate lien note – a contract between a borrower and a lender. See also *promissory note*.

real estate listing – See *listing*.

real estate market – the market in which real estate is sold.

real estate salesperson – See *sales associate*.

Real Estate Settlement Procedure Act (RESPA) – a federal law that deals with procedures to be follower in certain types of real estate closings.

real estate syndicate – a pooling of money by investors for the purchase of real estate investments.

real property – ownership rights in land and its improvements.

Real Property Administrator – professional designation for property managers.

real property sales contract – a contract for the purpose of selling real estate.

real savings – savings by persons and businesses that result from spending less than is earned.

real-cost inflation – higher prices due to greater effort needed to produce the same product today versus several years ago.

realtist – a member of the National Association of Real Estate Brokers, Inc.

REALTOR® – a registered trademark owned by the National Association of REALTORS® for use by its members.

REALTOR®-associate – a membership designation for salespersons working for REALTORS®.

realty – land and buildings and other improvements to land.

reasonable care – a requirement that an agent exhibit competence and expertise, keep clients informed, and take proper care of entrusted property.

rebars – steel reinforcement embedded in the concrete foundation.

rebate – a discount.

receiver – a manager appointed to take charge of property during the redemption period.

receptacle – connected to branch circuit wires that supply the current to equipment.

reciprocity – an arrangement whereby one state honors licenses issued by another state and vice versa.

reconveyance (release deed) – the return to the borrower of legal title upon repayment of the debt against the property.

record owner – the person named as the owner in public records.

recorded map – See *recorded plat*.

recorded plat – a subdivision map filed in the county recorder's office that shows the location and boundaries of individual parcels of land.

recorded survey – See *recorded plat*.

recording act – law that provides for the placing of documents in the public records.

recording fee – a fee paid at a government office or courthouse for the recording of real estate documents.

recourse financing – the investor is personally obligated to pay.

recovery fund – a state-operated fund that can be tapped to pay for uncollected judgments against real estate licensees.

rectangular survey system – a government system for surveying land that uses latitude and longitude lines as references.

red flag – something that would warn a reasonably observant person of an underlying problem.

redemption – a repurchase; a buying back. The process of canceling and annulling a defeasible title to land such as credited by a mortgage or tax sale by paying the debt or fulfilling other conditions.

redlining – a lender's practice of refusing to make loans in certain neighborhoods.

reentry – See *right of reentry*.

referee's deed in foreclosure – a deed issued as the result of a court-ordered foreclosure sale.

referral – recommending a business or a service by sending prospective clients.

referral fee – a fee that is received for referring and recommending a business or a service.

refinance – to pay a debt by making a another loan on new terms.

reformation – action taken to correct a mistake in a deed or other instrument.

reformation deed – See *correction deed*.

refrigerant – any substance that produces a cooling effect by absorbing heat as it vaporizes (disperses into the air).

regional shopping center – a large complex housing several national retail stores with a broad mix of shops that draw customers from a great distance.

registrar of titles – the preparer of a certification of title.

regular mortgage – a pledge of property to secure the repayment of a debt.

Regulation X – See *Real Estate Settlement Procedures Act*.

Regulation Z – See *Truth in Lending Act*.

reissue rate – reduced rate for title insurance if the previous owner's policy is available for updating.

REIT – See *Real Estate Investment Trust*.

relation back doctrine – a legal doctrine that has been applied to the escrow function relating to the time of performance. For example, when a document is given to an escrow officer for delivery to the grantee upon compliance with specified conditions, the date of delivery relates back to the time of deposit into escrow so as to constitute delivery to the grantee upon delivery to the escrow.

release deed – a document used to reconvey title from the trustee back to the property owner once the debt has been paid.

release of lien – an instrument indicating that a previously existing lien has been released and is no longer enforceable.

release of mortgage – a certificate from the lender stating that the loan has been repaid.

reliction – See *dereliction*.

remainder interest – an estate in land limited to take effect and be enjoyed after another estate has been terminated.

remainderman – one who is entitled to the remainder of the estate after a particular estate has expired.

remaining balance table – See *loan balance table*.

remise – to give up any existing claim one may have.

removal – covenant against.

rent – See *contract rent* and *economic rent*.

rent concession – the property owner keeps the rents at the same level, but offers a premium to entice a prospective tenant to move in.

rent control – government-imposed restrictions on the amount of rent a property owner can charge.

rental listing services – firms that specialize in finding rental units for tenants.

rental value – value of property expressed in terms of the right to its use for a specific period of time.

repairs – fixing or repairing a property.

replacement cost – the cost, at today's prices and using today's construction methods, of building an improvement having the same or equivalent usefulness as the subject property.

replacement value – value as measured by the current cost of building a structure of equivalent utility.

reproduction cost – the cost, at today's prices and using today's construction methods, of building an improvement having the same usefulness as the one being appraised.

request for notice of default – a notice filed requiring anyone holding a more senior lien to notify the junior mortgagee if a default notice has been filed.

resale certificate – common element disclosure certificate for condominiums.

rescind – cancel.

rescission – the annulling or unmaking of a contract.

reserve account (impound account) – an amount of money collected by a lender each month and reserved in an account so as to have enough to pay for property taxes and property insurance when they become due.

reserves for replacement – money set aside each year for the replacement of items that have a useful life greater than one year.

reservoir – a type of well-water storage that is generally used when a continuous but small supply of water is needed.

residence, sale of principal – the selling of the primary residence where a person lives.

resident manager – See *on-site management*.

Residential Lead-Based Paint Hazard Reduction Act – sets forth the procedures for disclosing the presence of lead-based paint in properties built prior to 1978.

residential property – a property for residential purpose.

residual – remainder, as the residual value of land after the economic life of the building is over.

resilient floor covering – a manufactured interior floor covering in either sheet or tile form that returns to its original form after being bent, compressed, or stretched.

resolution trust corporation (RTC) – a federal agency formed to liquidate insolvent savings and loans and banks.

resort timesharing – See *timesharing*.

RESPA – See *Real Estate Settlement Procedure Act*.

restitution – the act of restoring the situation to its status quo, or the equivalent thereof, for any loss, damage, or injury.

restrictive covenants – clauses placed in deeds and leases to control how future owners and lessees may or may not use the property.

restrictive report – a minimal report prepared by the appraiser.

retainage – a fund maintained by the owner or his agent, trustee, or receiver during the progress of construction or labor and service being performed by artisans and mechanics.

retaining walls – structures made from a variety of materials, such as brick, stone, slate, poured concrete, concrete block, and pressure-treated wood, that are used to hold back areas of earth.

retaliatory eviction – landlord evicts tenant because tenant has complained to authorities about the premises.

reverse mortgage – See *reverse annuity mortgage*.

reverse-annuity mortgage – the lender makes monthly payments to a homeowner who later repays in a lump sum.

reversionary interest – (1) the right to retake possession of a leased property at some future time; (2) the residue of the estate-usually the fee left to the grantor and his heirs after the termination of a particular estate that has been granted.

Revised Uniform Limited Partnership Act – recognition of the legality of limited partnerships and the requirement that they be formed by written documentation.

revocable – capable of being annulled or made void.

revocation – See *license revocation* and *notice of revocation*.

revoke – to take back or annul.

rider – any annexation to a document made part of the document by reference.

ridge beam – the highest part of the framing, it forms the apex, or top line, of the roof.

right of first refusal – the right to match or better an offer before the property is sold to someone else.

right of reentry – the right to resume the possession of lands in pursuance of a right that a party reserved to himself when he gave up his former possession or interest.

right of survivorship – a feature of joint tenancy whereby the surviving joint tenant automatically acquires all the right, title, and interest of the deceased joint tenant.

right-of-way – an easement allowing someone to use or travel over another person's land.

right-to-use – a contractual right to occupy a living unit at a timeshare resort.

riparian right – the right of a landowner whose land borders a river or stream to use and enjoy that water.

riparian water – water from a river or other body of water.

riser – the vertical area of the step that supports the tread.

rod – a survey measurement that is 16 1/2 feet long.

roof – the outside covering of the top of a building or structure.

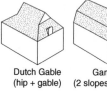

Dutch Gable
(hip + gable)

Gambrel
(2 slopes of gable)

roof shingle – See *shingle*.

roof tile – a roofing material, including clay tile styles, Spanish, French, and flat, which are

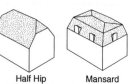

Half Hip
(hip + gable)

Mansard
(2 slopes of hip)

roof types

found in a variety of colors and can last in

excess of 75 years. Concrete tile is similar to clay tile in style; however, concrete tile weighs less and is less expensive. Concrete tiles can last up to 50 years. Certain concrete tiles hold up well in cold weather climates, while others are better suited for areas of the country without a freeze-thaw cycle.

roof truss system – See *truss*.

royalty – a payment to the owner or lessor of property usually involving a share of the product or profit made on that product extracted from the grantor's or lessor's property.

RTC – See *resolution trust corporation*.

rule against perpetuities – principle that no interest in property is good unless it must vest, if at all, no later than 21 years plus a period of gestation after some life or lives in being at the time of the creation of the interest.

Rule in Shelley's Case – a doctrine by which an ancestor takes an estate of freehold; in the same conveyance, the estate is limited to his heirs in fee or entail such that the estate is limited to only the heirs of that ancestor.

running with the land – land that moves with the title in any subsequent deed.

rural homestead – a homestead that is not in an urban area and can consist of not more than 200 acres.

R-value – the degree of resistance to heat transfer through the walls (heat is kept in or out); the larger the R-value, the greater the degree of insulation.

S

S Corporation – allows limited liability with profit-and-loss pass through.

S&L – See *Federal Savings and Loan Associations*.

safe harbor rule – a general rule that serves as an area of protection.

SAIF – See *savings association insurance fund*.

sale by advertisement – See *power of sale*.

sale-leaseback – a situation where the owner of a piece of property sells the property and retains occupancy by leasing it from the buyer.

sales approach – See *market comparison approach*.

sales associate – a licensed salesperson or broker employed by a broker to list, negotiate, sell, or lease real property for others.

sales contract – See *Statute of Frauds*.

salesperson – a person associated with a real estate broker for the purposes of performing acts or transactions comprehended by the term of Real Estate Broker as defined in the Texas Real Estate Licensing Act.

salvage value – the price that can be expected for an improvement that is to be removed and used elsewhere.

SAM – See *shared appreciation mortgage*.

satisfaction of mortgage – a certificate from the lender stating that the loan has been repaid.

satisfaction piece – an instrument that is recorded to announce payment of the debt; a mortgage release.

savings and loan association – a primary source of residential real estate loans.

savings association insurance fund (SAIF) – replaces the FSLIC fund that became insolvent due to failed thrifts. Insures savings and insured depositor's funds.

scarcity – shortage of land in a geographical area where there is a great demand for land.

scheduled gross (*also called* projected gross) – the estimated rent a fully occupied property can be expected to produce on an annual basis.

scratch coat – the first coat of gypsum plaster that is applied to the lath.

SE cable – See *service entrance cable*.

seal – a hot wax paper, or embossed seal, or the word *seal* or *L.S.* placed on a document.

seasoned loan – a loan on which payments have been made for one to two years or more.

second mortgage – a lien or encumbrance that ranks second in priority, right behind the first lien, mortgage, or encumbrance.

secondary financing – a second loan for the purchase of a property.

secondary industry – See *service industry*.

secondary mortgage market – a market in which mortgage loans can be sold to investors.

section – a unit of land in the rectangular survey system that is one mile long on each of its four sides and contains 640 acres.

Section 203 (b) – a section that describes the underwriting requirements for one of the FHA loans.

section joint – the area between garage door sections.

Securities and Exchange Commission – agency of the government that oversees and passes rules and regulations in furtherance of the Securities and Exchange Acts of 1933 and 1934.

securities license – a license needed when the property being sold is an investment contract in real estate rather than real estate itself.

security – a bond, note, investment contract, certificate of indebtedness, or other negotiable or transferable instrument evidencing debt or ownership.

security agreement – a form of chattel mortgage.

security deed – a warranty deed with a reconveyance clause.

security deposit – a deposit against which the manager can deduct for unpaid rent or damage to a building.

seepage pit – a covered pit through which the discharge from the septic tank infiltrates into the surrounding soil.

seisin – right of possession.

self-contained appraisal report – the most detailed report prepared by the appraiser.

seller – the owner who wants to sell his property.

seller financing – a note accepted by a seller instead of cash.

seller's affidavit of title – a document provided by the seller at the settlement meeting stating that he has done nothing to encumber title since the title search was made.

seller's closing statement – an accounting of the seller's money at settlement.

seller's market – one with few sellers and many buyers.

selling broker – See *buyer's broker*.

SEM – See *shared equity mortgage*.

senior mortgage – the mortgage against a property that holds first priority in the event of foreclosure.

separate property – the cubicle of airspace that the condominium owner's unit occupies;

spouse-owned property that is exempt from community property status.

septic system – a household wastewater treatment system consisting of a house sewer, septic tank, distribution box, and an absorption field or seepage pit.

service drop – aboveground cables that come from the nearest pole connecting to the service entrance conductors of the house or building.

service entrance (SE) cable – a single conductor or several conductors, with or without covering, used for aboveground service entrance.

service industry – an industry that produces goods and services to sell to local residents.

service lateral – electric service that runs underground.

service lateral conductors – conductors installed between the transformers and the meters for underground service.

service life – See *economic life*.

service the loan – to collect monthly payments and impounds, handle payoffs, releases, and delinquencies.

servient estate – an estate encumbered by an easement or servitude, which is reserved for the use of another.

setback requirements – specified distances from the front and interior property lines to the building.

settlement – See *title closing*.

settlement meeting – See *closing meeting*.

settlement statement – an accounting statement at settlement that shows each item charged or credited, to whom and for how much.

settlor – See *trustor*.

severable improvements – those improvements that can be removed without material injury to the real estate.

severalty ownership – an estate that is held by a person in his own right without any other person being joined or connected with him. See also *tenancy in severalty*.

severance damages – compensation paid for the loss in market value that results from splitting up a property in a condemnation proceeding.

shared appreciation mortgage (SAM) – typically offers an interest rate 1 to 2% below market rates.

shared equity mortgage (SEM) – a loan in which the lender or another party shares equity interest in the property.

shareholder (*also called* stockholder) – one who owns shares (one or more share) in a company stock.

shear panel – a floor, wall, or roof designed to serve as a deep beam to assist in stabilizing a building against deformation by lateral forces.

sheathing – a material, such as plywood, particle board, or gypsum board, used to cover exterior framing members.

sheriff's deed – a deed issued as a result of a court-ordered foreclosure sale.

sheriff's sale – a sale ordered by the court in which a sheriff or county official has the legal right to sell a distressed or foreclosed property. See also foreclosure.

Sherman Antitrust Act (1890) – federal law that condemns contracts, culmination, and conspiracies in restraint of trade and monopolizing, attempts to monopolize, and combinations and conspiracies to monopolize trade.

shifting executory use – a use that is so limited that it will be made to shift or transfer itself from one beneficiary to another upon the occurrence of a certain event after its creation. See also *contingent remainder*.

shingle – a roofing material that provides the waterproofing integrity for the roof.

shoring – bracing used to temporarily hold a wall in position.

sick building syndrome – a chemical illness that may be caused by the air quality inside a commercial building.

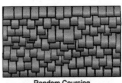

Random Coursing

Regular Coursing

arrangements of roof shingles

signature – acknowledgment.

sill plate – the first wooden member of the house and is used as the nailing surface for the floor system.

simple assumption – the property is sold and the loan is assumed by the buyer without notification to the FHA or its agent.

simple interest – interest paid on the declining balance of a loan; thus the interest payments lower as the principal amount is paid off.

simple interest – interest paid on the principal only; interest that is not compounded.

site – the location of a particular parcel of land.

site plan – a drawing of a construction site, showing the location of the building, contours of the land, and other features.

situs – refers to the preference by people for a given location.

skylight – a roof opening that is covered with a watertight transparent cover.

slab-on-grade construction – the foundation is a concrete slab instead of a foundation wall; the concrete slab is poured directly on the ground, eliminating the crawl space or basement.

slander of title – occurs when damaging, untrue, malicious and disparaging remarks about another person's title to a property are made to third parties.

slip form – a form designed to move upward as concrete is poured into it.

slope – land surface that is graded on an angle.

SMA – See *Systems Maintenance Administrator*.

Society of Real Estate Appraisers (SREA) – a professional organization with designation systems to recognize appraisal education, experience, and competence. Unified in 1991 with the American Institute of Real Estate Appraisers (AIREA) and renamed The Appraisal Institute, it is considered to provide the most highly respected designations in the industry.

soffit – the perforated area under the roof extension that allows air to flow through the ridge vents to ventilate the attic.

soil permeability – the ability of the soil to absorb water.

soil stacks – vertical pipes into which waste flows from waste pipes connected to each plumbing fixture.

solar energy – radiant energy originating from the sun.

sole control community property – community property that is subject to the sole control, management, or disposition of a single spouse that maintains all of its characteristics of community property.

sole ownership – See *severalty* ownership.

sole plate – a horizontal base plate that serves as the foundation for the wall system.

sole proprietorship – the simplest form of business organization that is owned by one individual and may use a name other than the owner's personal name.

solvents – liquids used in paint and other finishing materials that give the coating workability and that evaporate, permitting the finish material to harden.

spalling – the crumbling of brick.

special agency – an agency relationship created for the performance of specific acts only.

special assessment – a charge levied to provide publicly built improvements that will benefit a limited geographical area.

special exceptions – a use that is permitted within a certain zoning designation, but subject to control and supervision of the municipal authority.

special form (HO-3) – a policy that combines HO-5 coverage on the dwelling and HO-2 coverage on the personal property.

special lien – a lien on a specific property.

special use permit – allows use that is otherwise not permitted in a zone.

special warranty deed – a deed in which the grantor warrants or guarantees the title only against defects arising during his or her ownership of the property and not against defects existing before the time of ownership.

specific lien – a lien on a specific property.

specific performance – contract performance according to the precise terms agreed upon.

specific property offering – property purchase method whereby the organizers buy properties first and then seek partners; the prospective limited partner knows in advance what properties will be owned.

specifications – text setting forth details such as description, size, quality, performance, workmanship, and so forth. Specifications that pertain to all of the construction trades involved might be subdivided into "General Conditions" and "Supplemental General Conditions." Further subdividing the specifications might be specific requirements for the various contractors such as electrical, plumbing, heating, masonry, and so forth.

splitting fees – the act of sharing commissions between brokers.

spot zoning – a specific property within a zoned area is rezoned to permit a use different from the zoning requirements for that area; it is illegal in many states.

springing executory use – a use limited to arise on future event in which no preceding use is limited. It does not take effect in derogation of any interest of the grantor, and remains in the grantor in the meantime. See also *fee on condition precedent.*

square – in roofing, 100 square feet of roofing material.

square-foot method – an appraisal technique that uses square-foot construction costs of similar structures as an estimating basis.

SREA – See *Society of Real Estate Appraisers.*

standard mortgage – a pledge of property to secure the repayment of a debt.

standard parallel – a survey line used to correct for the earth's curvature.

standards of practice – interpretations of various articles in the code of ethics.

standby fee – fees paid to an investor for holding funds.

starter – a device used in conjunction with a ballast for the purpose of starting an electric discharge lamp.

state district courts – state civil courts with no dollar-limit jurisdiction.

state test – test containing questions regarding laws, rules, regulations, and practices of the jurisdiction where the test is being given.

Statue of Frauds – a law requiring that certain types of contracts, such as those pertaining to real estate, be written in order to be enforceable in a court of law.

statute – a law passed by the legislative body of government.

statute of limitations – a legal limit on the amount of time one has to seek the aid of a court in obtaining justice.

statutory dedication – conveyance through the approval and recordation of a subdivision map.

statutory estates – estates created by law and including dower, curtesy, community property, and homestead rights.

statutory foreclosure – foreclosure per legislative law.

statutory law – law created by the enactment of legislation.

statutory lien – a lien imposed on a property under statutory law.

statutory retainage – See *retainage*.

statutory right of redemption – the right of a borrower after a foreclosure sale to reclaim his property by repaying the defaulted loan.

steam system – a heating system that consists of a boiler, where steam is produced, and a system of pipes that conveys the steam to radiators, convectors, or other types of room-heating elements.

steering – the illegal practice of directing home seekers to particular neighborhoods based on race, color, religion, sex, national origin, or handicapped or adults-only status.

step-up rental – See *graduated rental*.

stile – side framing member of the window sash.

straight-line depreciation – depreciation in equal amounts each year over the life of the asset.

straw man – person who purchases for another unidentified buyer; used when confidentiality is important.

street numbers – as a means of describing property.

strict foreclosure – the lender acquires absolute title without the need for a foreclosure sale.

stringer – also known as the carriage, it supports the stairway.

strip center – a building consisting of a number of units (bays) conveniently located near main arteries.

stucco – a portland cement plaster used as the finish material on building exteriors.

studs – framing members, commonly 2 3 4s, 2 3 8s, 2 3 10s, or 2 3 12s, used vertically for wall construction.

sub-agency – created by two or more independent brokers representing the principal; the first broker being the primary agent and the second broker being the subagent.

subagent – an agent appointed by one who is himself an agent, or a person employed by an agent, to assist in transacting the affairs of the principal.

Subchapter S – the liability protection of a corporation with the profit-and-loss pass-through of a partnership.

subcontractor – a contractor who has a direct contractual relationship and works under an original contractor. He has no direct contractual relationship with the owner of the property or his agent.

subdivider – a person who divides undeveloped land into smaller lots for the purpose of development.

subdivision land – land that is divided into lots for development purposes.

subdivision map – See *recorded plat*.

subfloor – a plywood surface nailed to the floor joists that serves as the surface for the floor finish.

subject property – the property that is being appraised.

subject to the existing loan – said of property that is bought subject to the existing loan against it; the buyer makes the payments but does not take personal responsibility for the loan.

sublease – a lease given by a lessee to a sublessee for a part of the premises or for a period of time less than the remaining term of the lessee's original lease.

sublessee – one who rents from a lessee.

sublessor – a lessee who rents to another lessee.

sublet – to transfer only a portion of one's lease rights.

submergence – See *subsidence*.

subordination – voluntary acceptance of a lower mortgage priority than one would otherwise be entitled to.

subpoena – a legal summons requiring court appearance to give testimony.

subprime loan – a loan with risk-based pricing for persons who have poor credit or fail to qualify for prime, conventional loans. Usually a rate is found, or negotiated, if it fits the risk profile. Interest rates are typically one to five percentage points higher than for good credit risks. With these loans, appraisals are critical and the risk profiles tend to be variable from lender to lender. Subprime lenders are largely unregulated by the federal government.

subrogation – the substitution of one person in the place of another with reference to a lawful claim, demand, or right.

subsidence – when water advances to cover the previously dry land.

substitution, principle of – maximum value of a property in the marketplace tends to be set by the cost of purchasing an equally desirable substitute property provided no costly delay in encountered making the substitution.

subsurface right – the right of the owner to use land below the earth's surface.

sufferance – See *tenancy at sufferance*.

summary report – a summarized report prepared by the appraiser.

summons – notification to appear in court.

sunk cost – a cost already incurred that is not subject to revision.

Superfund Amendment and Reauthorization Act of 1986 – a federal law that creates a lien in favor of the United States upon property subject to or affected by hazardous substance removal or remedial action by the superfund statute. This statute puts liability for cleanup of the site on: (1) the owner and operator of the facility, (2) the person who operates the facility, and (3) the person who arranges for disposal or the transportation of materials to that facility.

superintendent – See *on-site management*.

supervening illegality – one of the methods to terminate an agency.

supervisory broker – See *principal broker*.

supply and demand – refers to the ability of people to pay for land coupled with the relative scarcity of land.

Supreme Court of the United States – the highest court to which any cases can be appealed in the United States.

surety bond – a form of insurance purchased as security against loss or damage.

surface right – the right of the property owner to use the surface of a parcel of land. See also *dominant estate*.

surface right of entry – surface right for the purpose of entering land.

surface runoff – the loss of water from an area by its flow over the land's surface.

surplus money action – a claim for payment filed by a junior mortgage holder at a foreclosure sale.

surrogate court – See *probate court*.

survey books – map books.

survivorship, right of – a feature of joint tenancy whereby the surviving joint tenant automatically acquires all the rights, title, and interest of the deceased joint tenant. See also *joint tenancy*.

suspend – to temporarily make ineffective.

swing loan – See *bridge loan*.

switch – used to open and close electrical circuits and allow current to flow to appliances.

syndication (syndicate) – a group of persons or businesses that combine to undertake an investment.

Systems Maintenance Administrator (SMA) – professional designation for property managers.

T

T intersection – the intersection of one street into another, thus forming a "T."

T lot – a lot at the end of a T intersection.

tack on – adding successive periods of continuous occupation to qualify for title by adverse possession.

tacking – adding successive periods of continuous occupation to qualify for title by adverse possession.

take-out loan – a permanent loan arranged to replace a construction loan.

taking – where the municipality regulates the property to where it has no value or, in some cases, no remaining economic value.

taking back paper – said of a seller who allows a purchaser to substitute a promissory note for cash.

tax assessment – a levy against property to pay for a public improvement that benefits the real estate.

tax basis – the price paid for a property plus certain costs and expenses. See also *basis*.

tax benefits – savings by cash credits or tax deductible items.

tax certificate – a document issued at a tax sale that entitles the purchaser to a deed at a later date if the property is not redeemed.

tax credit – reduces tax savings dollar for dollar.

tax deed – a document that conveys title to property purchased at a tax sale.

tax deferred exchange – provision in tax law that allows for the exchange of "like kind" property; a sale of real property in exchange for another parcel of real estate, to affect a non-taxable gain.

tax lien – a charge or hold by the government against property to insure the payment of taxes.

tax rate – rate for ad valorem taxes, expressed as dollars per hundred, set by elected officials.

Tax Reform Act – See *Internal Revenue Code of 1986*.

tax roll – a pubic list of taxable properties.

tax sale – sale made pursuant to state law to satisfy a debt created by delinquent taxes.

tax shelter – the income tax savings that an investment can produce for its owner.

taxation – one of the inherent burdens on private ownership of land; property taxes constitute a specific lien against the real estate.

taxes – covenant to pay.

tax-free exchange – See *tax-deferred exchange*.

T-bill – a government treasury bill.

TDR – See *transferable development right*.

teaser rate – an adjustable loan with an initial rate below the market.

temperature pressure relief valve – used in hot water and steam systems, it allows hot water and steam to escape if the water temperature and pressure buildup are too high for the equipment.

tenancy – the estate of a tenant whether it be in fee, for life, for years, at will, or otherwise.

tenancy at sufferance – occurs when a tenant stays beyond his legal tenancy without the consent of the landlord.

tenancy at will – tenancy without a specific period of possession that occurs at the will and consent of the owner.

tenancy by the entirety – a form of joint ownership reserved for married persons; right of survivorship exists and neither spouse has a disposable interest during the lifetime of the other.

tenancy for life – See *life estate and tenancy*.

tenancy for years – a leasehold estate that grants the lessee use for a specified period of time.

tenancy in common – shared ownership of a single property among two or more persons; interests need not be equal and no right of survivorship exists.

tenant – one who has the temporary use and occupation of real property owned by another person (called the "landlord"). The duration and terms of his or her tenancy usually are fixed by law or by an instrument called a lease.

Tenant's form (HO-4) – an insurance policy designed for residential tenants.

tender – to fulfill; to offer to perform as the terms of a contract state.

term – the length of time agreed upon.

term loan – a loan requiring interest-only payments until the maturity date (due date) at which time the entire principal is due.

termite – a type of insect that eats wood.

termite inspection – inspection for wood destroying insects by a licensed professional.

termite report – an official report on the inspection of wood destroying insects on a subject property.

testament – the final legal document disposing of a person's property after death or by a will.

testamentary trust – a trust that takes effect after death.

testate – to die with a last will and testament.

testator – a person who makes a will (masculine), testatrix (feminine).

tester – an individual or organization that responds to advertising and visits real estate offices to test for compliance with fair housing laws.

testimony clause – a declaration in a document that reads, "In witness whereof the parties hereto set their hands and seals" or a similar phrase.

thermocouple – a device that automatically closes the gas valve that controls the flow of gas and stops its flow if the pilot light goes out.

thermostat – a control device that automatically responds to temperature changes by opening and closing an electric circuit.

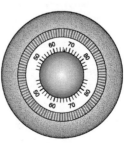

thermostat

thin market – a market with few buyers and few sellers.

third party – a person who is not a party to a contract but who may be affected by it.

threshold – the area on the ground in front of the door that keeps rain and snow from entering the structure.

throat damper – a damper located in the throat of the fireplace, just above the firebox.

tidelands – offshore land within the territorial water of the state.

Tiebacks Component – of a wood retaining wall; must be anchored to the soil to prevent collapse of the wall.

tight money – loan money is in short supply and loans are hard to get.

tile – See *clay tile* and *roof tile*.

time is of the essence – a phrase that means that the time limits of a contract must be faithfully observed or the contract is voidable.

timeshare condominiums – condominiums that are owned among several co-tenants who have the right, by contractual agreement with each other, to use the condominium only for a certain time period (usually from two to four weeks). This time period may change from year to year depending upon the arrangement of the co-tenants' contractual agreement.

timeshare system – a cooperative system between timeshare condominiums to share occupancy times between the respective unit owners.

timesharing – part ownership of a property coupled with a right to exclusive use of it for a specified number of days per year.

title – the right to or ownership of something; the evidence of ownership such as a deed or bill of sale.

title by descent – laws that direct how a deceased's assets shall be divided when there is no will.

title by prescription – See *adverse possession*.

title closing – the process of completing a real estate transaction.

title cloud – See *cloud on the title.*

title commitment – a statement of the current condition of title for a parcel of land; obligates the title insurance company to issue a policy of title when curative requirement have been satisfied.

title defect – See *cloud on the title.*

title insurance – an insurance policy against defects in title not listed in the title report or abstract.

title plant – a duplicate set of public records maintained by a title company.

title report – See *title commitment.*

title search – an inspection of publicly available records and documents to determine the current ownership and title condition for a property.

title searcher – a person who searches the public records.

title theory – the legal position that a mortgage conveys title to the lender.

topographical survey – a survey by means of contour lines.

topography – includes types of soil; the location of water such as wetlands, springs, or floodplains; forest areas; and the location of rocks, trees, and other vegetation.

torrens system – a state-sponsored method of registering land titles.

torsion springs – usually mounted above the closed garage door, parallel and horizontal to the top section of the door, they provide lifting power by winding and unwinding while the door is opened or closed.

tort – an actionable wrong, a violation of a legal right.

total payments – the amount in dollars the borrower will have paid after making all the payments scheduled.

townhouse – a dwelling unit usually with two or three floors and shared walls; usually found in PUDs.

township – a six-by-six-mile square of land designated by the intersection of range lines and township lines in the rectangular survey system.

toxic substance – an element capable of causing adverse human health or environmental effects through exposure to even low levels.

tract – an area of land.

tract index – a system for listing recorded documents affecting a particular tract of land.

trade fixtures – such chattels as merchants usually possess and annex to the premises occupied by them to enable them to store, handle, and display their goods, which are generally removable without material injury to the premises at the termination of the lease.

transferable – to move a good or service to another person.

transferable development right (TDR) – a legal means by which the right to develop a particular parcel of land can be transferred to another parcel.

transformer – used to change alternating current from one voltage to another.

trap – a curved section of drainpipe that fills with water and provides a seal that prevents sewer gasses from entering a structure.

tread – the horizontal surface of the stair.

treasury bonds – interest-bearing bonds of $1,000 or more issued by the u.s. government and that mature in 10 to 30 years.

treasury notes – interest-bearing notes of $1,000 or more issued by the u.s. treasury and that mature in 10 years or less.

treble damages – court awarded damages of three times the actual amount.

trigger terms – credit advertising that requires compliance with truth-in-lending rules.

trim – made of either metal or wood and used to finish windows, doorways, cabinetry, shelving, and the areas where the floor meets the wall and the wall meets the ceiling.

tri-party agreements – agreements to loan money involving the construction financing lender, the permanent lender, and the borrower. Each promises to undertake a certain phase of financing a construction project.

triple net lease – See *net lease*.

triplex – a building with three units.

trust – a right of property held by one party for the benefit of another.

truss – a roof frame made up of a number of smaller framing members; it carries the load-bearing function to the outer walls.

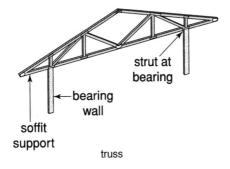

truss

trust account – a separate account for holding clients' and customers' money.

trust deed – See *deed of trust*.

trustee – one who holds property in trust for another.

trustee's deed – See *sheriff's deed*.

trustor (*also called* settlor) – one who creates a trust; the borrower in a deed of trusts arrangement.

Truth in Lending Act – a federal law that requires certain disclosures when extending or advertising credit.

Truth-in-Lending Act – a federal statute that requires disclosure of specific loan information to the borrower before the obligation becomes effective.

turnkey – a finished product, ready for delivery or installation.

U

U.S. Code Annotated – volumes that contain the annotated federal statutes, rulings, decisions rendered, and positions taken by governmental agencies, interpreting law and regulations under their jurisdictions.

U.S. public land survey – a system for surveying land that uses latitude and longitude lines as references.

UBC – See *Uniform Building Code*.

UCC lien – lien which attaches pursuant to the provisions of the Uniform Commercial Code.

UFFI – See *urea formaldehyde foam insulation*.

UFMIP – See *up-front mortgage insurance premium*.

unconscionable bargain – a bargain that no man in his right senses would make and that no fair and honest man would accept because of unfairness to the other.

underground storage tanks – used for the bulk storage of chemicals and petroleum.

underwrite – to insure; to assume liability to the extent of a specified sum.

underwriter – the person who reviews a loan application and makes recommendation to the loan committee concerning the risk and desirability of making the loan.

undisclosed agency – when agency relationship is not clearly identified.

undivided interest – ownership by two or more persons that gives each the right to use the entire property.

undue influence – unfair advantage to obtain a contract.

unearned income – passive income.

unenforceable contract – a contract whose enforcement is barred by the statute of limitations or the doctrine of laches.

unfair and deceptive practices – fraudulent, misleading business practices that involve the general public or competing parties that is prohibited by statute and/or regulated by a government agency.

Uniform Building Code (UBC) – one of the family of codes and related publications published by the International Conference of Building Officials (ICBO) and other organizations, such as the International Association of Plumbing and Mechanical Officials (IAPMO) and the National Fire Protection Association (NFPA), designed to be compatible with other codes, as together they make up the enforcement tools of a jurisdiction.

Uniform Commercial Code – code that requires that the sale of personal property with value in excess of $500 be in writing.

Uniform Partnership Act – an act that introduces clarity and uniformity into general partnership laws.

uniform residential appraisal report (URAR) – a report produced by professional appraisers that supports the estimated value of a property.

uniform settlement statement – complete settlement charges for both the buyer and the seller.

Uniform Standards of Professional Appraisal Practice (USPAP) – mandatory requirements for certain federally related real estate appraisals.

uniform test – test containing questions relevant to the principles and practices of real estate that are uniform across the country.

unilateral contract – results when a promise is exchanged for performance.

unilateral rescission – innocent party refuses to perform his or her contractual duties because the other party has not performed.

unimproved property – raw land.

unincorporated area – rural areas not incorporate by a municipality.

unincorporated non-profit association – an unincorporated organization, other than one created by a trust, consisting of three or more persons joined by mutual consent for a common, non-profit purpose.

unit deed – a deed to a condominium unit.

United States geographical survey (USGS) – one of the three commonly used major surveying systems.

unities – See *four unities of a joint tenancy*.

unit-in-place method – an appraisal technique that calculates the cost of all the component parts to be used in the construction to arrive at the value.

unity of interest – all joint tenants own one interest together.

unity of person – the legal premise that husband and wife are an indivisible legal unit and a requirement of tenancy by the entirety.

unity of possession – all co-tenants must enjoy the same undivided possession of the whole property.

unity of time – each joint tenant must acquire his or her ownership interest at the same moment.

unity of title – all joint tenants must acquire their interest from the same deed or will.

universal agency – an agency wherein the agent is empowered to transact matters of all types for the principal.

unjust enrichment – the doctrine that persons shall not be allowed to profit to enrich themselves inequitably at another's expense.

unmarketable title – title that is not clear as to who is the owner.

up-front mortgage insurance premium (UFMIP) – a one-time charge by the FHA for insuring a loan.

URAR – See *uniform residential appraisal report*.

urban homestead – a homestead in an urban area, which can consist of a lot or lots not to exceed one acre at the time of designation.

urea formaldehyde foam insulation (UFFI) – a type of foam containing formaldehyde used as home insulation until the early 1980s.

USGS – See *United States geographical survey*.

USPAP – See *Uniform Standards of Professional Appraisal Practice*.

usury – charging a rate of interest higher than that permitted by law.

utility – the ability of a good or service to fill demand.

utility easement – the right held by a utility company to make use of a utility easement on a person's property.

V

VA – See *Veterans Administration loan*.

vacant land – land without buildings, but not necessarily without improvements including utilities and sewers.

valid contract – one that meets all require-ments of law, is binding upon its parties, and is enforceable in a court of law.

valley – the intersection of two inclined sur-faces.

valuable consideration – money, property, services, forbearance, or anything worth money.

valuation of real property – See *appraisal*.

valve – a device used to regulate the flow of a liquid or gas; it may force the flow in a certain direction.

vapor barrier – sheets of moisture-resistant material, such as polyethylene film, kraft paper, or aluminum foil, bonded to insulation that pre-vent warm interior air from mixing with cold exterior air and forming condensation within the wall.

variable interest rate (VIR) or variable mort-gage rate (VMR) – an interest rate that adjusts at a predetermined time based on a pubic index.

variable rate mortgage (VRM) – a mortgage on which the interest rate rises and falls with changes in prevailing interest rates.

variance – a permit granted to an individual property owner to vary slightly from strict compliance with zoning requirements.

vassals – tenants of the lord and subtenants of the kind.

vendee – the buyer.

vendor – the seller.

vendor's lien – a lien implied to belong to a vendor for the unpaid purchase price of the land.

veneer – a thin sheet of material used to cover another surface.

vent system – a system of pipes that provides a flow of air to and from a drainage system; it permits gases and odors to circulate up through the system and escape into the air.

ventilation – a system for replacing stale air with fresh or conditioned air in various places inside a structure where pollutant concentrations are usually highest (attics, bathrooms, kitchens).

venue – at law, a county or jurisdiction in which an actual prosecution is brought for trial, and which is to furnish a panel of jurors. Also, it relates to the territory within which a matter has jurisdiction to be performed or completed.

vested – owned by.

vested remainder – a remainderman whose estate is invariably fixed to remain to that determined person after the prior estate has expired.

Veterans Administration loan – a loan partially guaranteed by the Veterans Administration.

VIR – See *variable interest rate*.

VMR – See *variable interest rate*.

void – having no legal force or effect.

void contract – a contract that has no binding effect on the parties who made it.

voidable – a contract that appears valid and forcible on its face but is subject to rescission by one of the parties because of its latent defect.

voidable contract – a contract that binds one party but gives the other the right to withdraw.

volt – the difference of electric potential between two points of a conductor carrying a constant current of one ampere, when the power dissipated between these points is equal to one watt. A voltage can push one ampere through a resistance of one OHM.

voltage – the electrical pressure that pushes through wires.

voluntary deed – See *deed in lieu of foreclosure*.

voluntary lien – a lien created by the property owner.

W

waive – to surrender or give up.

waiver – the voluntary surrender of rights or claims.

walk-through – a final inspection of the property just prior to settlement.

warehouse – a building used for storing merchandise.

warranty – an assurance or guarantee that something is true as stated.

warranty deed – a deed that usually contains the covenants of seizin, quiet enjoyment, encumbrances, further assurance, and warranty forever.

warranty forever – the grantor's guarantee to bear the expense of defending the grantee's title.

waste – abuse or destructive use of property.

water erosion – the removal of soil material by flowing water.

water hammer arrestor – a type of valve that contains a hydraulic piston that absorbs the shock waves produced by sudden changes in water flow; it reduces the commonly heard banging in pipes.

water right – the right to use water on or below or bordering a parcel of land.

water table – the uppermost boundary of the groundwater.

waterfront property – property adjacent to a large body of water.

waterproofing – material used to make a surface impervious to the penetration of water.

water-repellent – liquid that penetrates the pores of wood and prevents moisture from penetrating without altering the desirable qualities of the wood.

watt – the power required to do work at the rate of 1 joule per second. Wattage is determined by multiplying voltage times amperes times the power factor of the circuit: $W = E \times 1 \times PF$.

weepholes – small perforations in retaining wall material that allow water drainage.

well-water storage tank – a tank used to prevent the well from pumping every time the household uses water. Types of well-water storage include pressure tanks, elastic pressure cells, gravity cells, gravity tanks, and reservoirs.

wetlands – federal- and state-protected transition areas between uplands and aquatic habitats that provide flood and storm water control, surface and groundwater protection, erosion control, and pollution treatment.

will – a formal or witness document, prepared in most cases by an attorney, that protects a deceased's intentions with regard to his or her property and possessions after his or her death. A will must meet specific legal requirements and the testator must declare it to be his or her will and sign it in the presence of two to four witnesses (depending on the state), who, at the testator's request and in the presence of each other, sign the will as witnesses.

window sash – the frame that surrounds and secures the glass of a window.

window sill – the horizontal bottom part of a window frame.

window trim – See *trim*.

witnessed will – a formal will that is normally prepared by an attorney and properly witnessed according to statute.

wood rot – caused by a type of fungus that destroys wood; it is as damaging as termite or other insect infestation.

wood-destroying insect – an insect capable of causing wood structure damage.

words of conveyance – the grantor's statement of making a grant to the grantee.

worker's compensation insurance – insurance for injuries to workers while on the job.

worst-case scenario – shows what can happen to the borrower's payments if the index rises to its maximum in an adjustable loan.

wraparound deed of trust – See *wraparound mortgage*.

wraparound mortgage – a mortgage that encompasses any existing mortgages and is subordinate to them.

writ of attachment – a legal seizure of property issued by judges and clerks of the district and county courts to prevent alienation of real property pending a judicial proceeding.

writ of execution – a court document directing the county sheriff to seize and sell a debtor's property.

writ of possession – a writ issued by a court of competent jurisdiction commanding a sheriff to restore the premises to the true owner.

wythe – a solid brick partition in the flue.

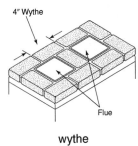

4″ Wythe

Flue

wythe

Y

year-to-year tenancy – tenancy that is based from one year to the next without a contract or lease.

yield – See *effective yield*.

Z

zero lot line – the placing of a structure on the lot line without being required to have a setback from the perimeter of the property.

zoning – public regulations that control the specific use of land in a given district.

zoning commissioners – those appointed by a city council to review and enforce the city's zoning ordinance.

zoning ordinance – a statement setting forth the type of use permitted under each zoning classification and the specific requirements for compliance.

zoning variance – the limited changes allowed without changing the character of the zoned area.

Appendices

The Basic Structure of a House

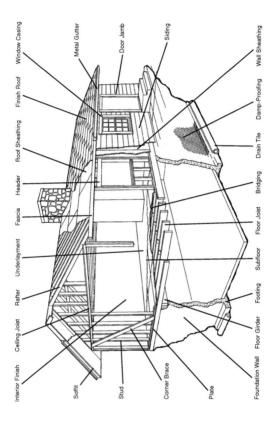

Source: Spada, Marcia Darvin, *The Home Inspection Book: A Guide for Professionals*. Cincinnati, OH: South-Western Publishing. 2002. Reprinted with permission.

Construction Illustrations and Terminology

Combined Slab and Foundation
(Thickened Edge Slab)

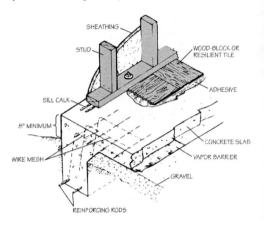

Basement Details

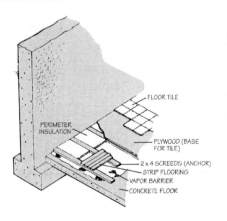

Source: Jacobus, Charles J., *Real Estate Principles,* Ninth Edition. Cincinnati, OH: South-Western Publishing. 2003. Reprinted with permission.

Floor Framing

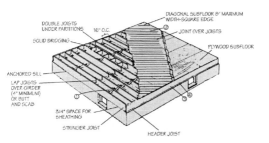

Wall Framing Used with Platform Construction

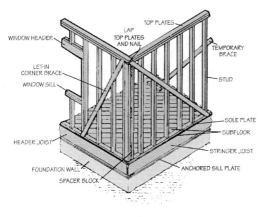

Source: Jacobus, Charles J., *Real Estate Principles,* Ninth Edition. Cincinnati, OH: South-Western Publishing. 2003. Reprinted with permission.

Construction Illustrations and Terminology / Continued

Headers for Windows and Door Openings

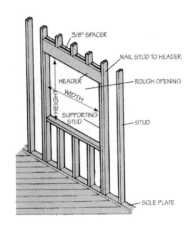

Vertical Application of Plywood or Structural Insulation Board Sheathing

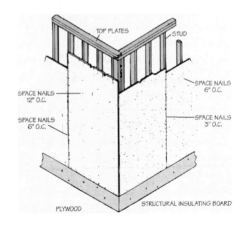

Source: Jacobus, Charles J., *Real Estate Principles,* Ninth Edition. Cincinnati, OH: South-Western Publishing. 2003. Reprinted with permission.

Exterior Siding

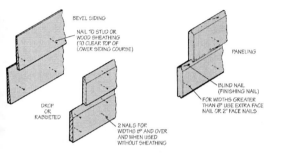

Vertical Board Siding

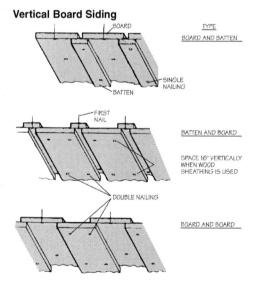

Source: Jacobus, Charles J., *Real Estate Principles,* Ninth Edition. Cincinnati, OH: South-Western Publishing. 2003. Reprinted with permission.

Construction Illustrations and Terminology / Continued

Application of Gypsum Board Finish

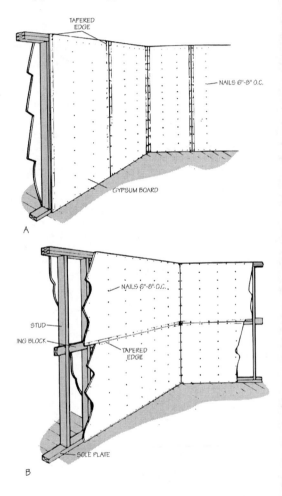

Application of Insulation

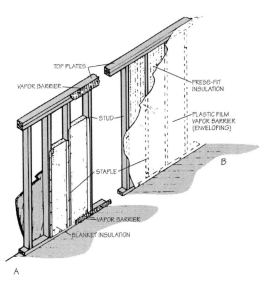

TOP PLATES

VAPOR BARRIER

PRESS-FIT INSULATION

STUD

PLASTIC FILM VAPOR BARRIER (ENVELOPING)

STAPLE

B

VAPOR BARRIER

BLANKET INSULATION

A

Construction Illustrations and Terminology / Continued

Masonry Fireplace

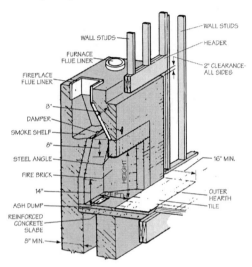

Stairway Detail

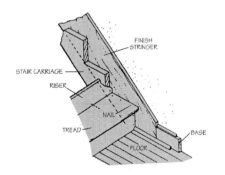

Source: Jacobus, Charles J., *Real Estate Principles,* Ninth Edition. Cincinnati, OH: South-Western Publishing. 2003. Reprinted with permission.

Door Details

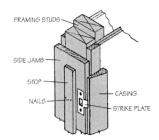

Ceiling and Roof Framing

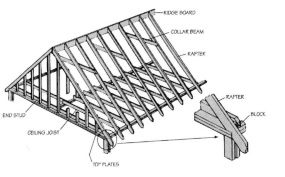

Source: Jacobus, Charles J., *Real Estate Principles,* Ninth Edition. Cincinnati, OH: South-Western Publishing. 2003. Reprinted with permission.

Construction Illustrations and Terminology / Continued

Installation of Board Roof Sheathing, Showing Both Closed and Spaced Types

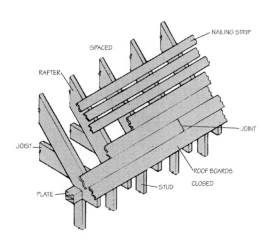

Built-up Roof

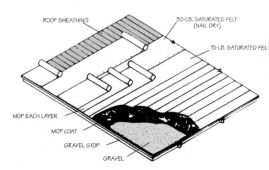

Source: Jacobus, Charles J., *Real Estate Principles,* Ninth Edition. Cincinnati, OH: South-Western Publishing. 2003. Reprinted with permission.

Construction Illustrations and Terminology

Application of Asphalt Shingles

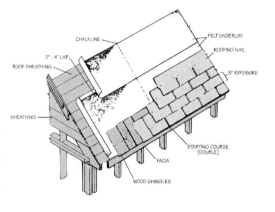

Source: Jacobus, Charles J., *Real Estate Principles,* Ninth Edition. Cincinnati, OH: South-Western Publishing. 2003. Reprinted with permission.

Forms of Ownership

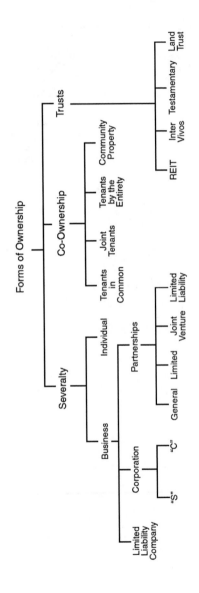

Source: Jacobus, Charles J., *Real Estate Principles*, Ninth Edition. Cincinnati, OH: South-Western Publishing. 2003. Reprinted with permission.

Concurrent Ownership by State	L.L.P.*	L.L.C.**	Tenancy in common	Joint tenancy	Tenancy by the entirety	Community property
Alabama	X	X	X	X		
Alaska		X	X	X	X	X
Arizona	X	X	X	X		X
Arkansas		X	X	X	X	
California		X	X	X		X
Colorado		X	X	X		
Connecticut		X	X	X		
Delaware	X	X	X	X	X	
District of Columbia	X	X	X	X	X	
Florida		X	X	X	X	
Georgia	X	X	X	X		
Hawaii		X	X	X	X	
Idaho	X	X	X	X		X
Illinois		X	X	X		
Indiana		X	X	X	X	
Iowa	X	X	X	X		
Kansas	X	X	X	X		
Kentucky		X	X	X	X	
Louisiana	X	X				X
Maine		X	X	X		
Maryland	X	X	X	X	X	
Massachusetts		X	X	X	X	
Michigan	X	X	X	X	X	
Minnesota	X	X	X	X		
Mississippi	X	X	X	X	X	

continued

Concurrent Ownership by State/ continued

	L.L.P.*	L.L.C.**	Tenancy in common	Joint tenancy	Tenancy by the entirety	Community property
Missouri		X	X	X	X	
Montana		X	X	X		
Nebraska		X	X	X		
Nevada		X	X	X		X
New Hampshire		X	X	X		
New Jersey	X	X	X	X	X	
New Mexico		X	X	X		X
New York		X	X	X	X	
North Carolina	X	X	X	X	X	
North Dakota		X	X	X		
Ohio	X	X	X		X	
Oklahoma		X	X	X	X	
Oregon		X	X		X	
Pennsylvania		X	X	X	X	
Rhode Island		X	X	X	X	
South Carolina		X	X	X		
South Dakota		X	X	X		
Tennessee		X	X	X	X	
Texas	X	X	X	X		X
Utah	X	X	X	X	X	
Vermont		X	X	X	X	
Virginia	X	X	X	X	X	
Washington		X	X	X		X
West Virginia		X	X	X	X	
Wisconsin		X	X	X		X
Wyoming		X	X	X	X	

Source: Jacobus, Charles J., *Real Estate Principles,* Ninth Edition. Cincinnati, OH: South-Western Publishing. 2003. Reprinted with permission.

English-Spanish Key

Abstract	Compendio
Abstract of Title	Compendio del título
Abstractor	Abstractor
Accelerated depreciation	Depreciación acelerada
Acceleration clause	Provisión para vencimiento anticipado
Accession	Accesión
Accretion	Acrecencia
Acknowledgment	Reconocimiento
Acre	Acre
Actual notice	Notificación efectiva
Ad valorem taxes	Impuestos al valor
Adjustable rate mortgage	Hipoteca con tasa ajustable
Adjusted market price	Precio ajustado del mercado
Adjusted sales price	Precio de venta ajustado
Administrator (administratrix)	Administrador (administradora)
Adverse possession	Prescripción adquisitiva
Agency	Agencia
Agency by estoppel	Agencia por impedimento
Agency by ratification	Agencia por ratificación
Agency coupled with an interest	Agencia aunada a un interés
Agent	Agente
Agreement of sale. See installment contract	Convenio de venta. Vea contrato a plazo
Air lot	Lote aéreo
Air right	Derecho aéreo
Alienation clause	Cláusula de enajenación
Alienation of title	Enajenación de título
Allodial system	Sistema alodial
Alluvion	Aluvión
Amendatory language	Lenguaje enmendatorio, correctivo
Americans with Disabilities Act (ADA)	Ley sobre Estadounidenses Incapacitados
Amortized loan	Préstamo amortizado
Amount financed	Cantidad financiada
Amount realized	Cantidad realizada
Annual percentage rate	Tasa de porcentaje anual

Anticipation, principle of	Principio de anticipación
Apartment locators	Empresa localizadora de apartamentos
Appraisal	Avalúo
Appraisal letter	Carta de avalúo
Appraisal review board	Junta revisora de avalúos
Appraise	Avaluar
Appraiser	Valuador
Appreciation	Apreciación
Appropriation process	Proceso de apropiación
Appurtenance	Pertenencia
As-is	Como está
Assemblage	Agrupación
Assessed district. See Improvement district	Distrito avaluado. Vea Distrito de mejoras
Assessed Value	Valor catastral
Assessment roll	Registro de avalúos
Asset integrated mortgage	Hipoteca integrada con activo
Assign	Ceder
Assignee	Cesionario
Assignment	Cesión
Association	Asociación
Association dues	Cuotas de asociación
Assumed loan	Préstamo adquirido
At risk	En riesgo
Attorney-in-fact	Apoderado
Automated underwriting systems	Sistema automático de subscripción
Avulsion	Avulsión
Balloon loan	Préstamo de saldo mayor
Balloon payment	Pago de saldo mayor
Banks	Bancos
Bargain and sale deed	Escritura de compraventa
Base line	Línea base de demarcación
Basis	Base
Benchmark	Punto de referencia
Beneficial Interest	Interés beneficial
Beneficiary	Beneficiario
Bequest	Legado
Bilateral contract	Contrato bilateral
Bill of sale	Documento de venta

Blanket mortgage	Hipoteca colectiva
Blended-rate loan	Préstamo de taza combinada
Blind pool	Consorcio a ciegas
Blockbusting	Rompe cuadras
Blue-sky laws	Leyes cielo azul
Borrower's points	Puntos de prestatario
Boycotting	Boicot
Breach of contract	Incumplimiento del contrato
Broad market	Mercado extenso
Broker	Corredor
Budget mortgage	Hipoteca módica
Buffer zone	Zona amortiguadora
Building codes	Reglamentos de construcción
Buyer's broker	Corredor representante del comprador
Buyer's market	Mercado de comprador
Buyer's walk-through	Inspección del comprador
Bylaws	Estatutos
Call clause (due on sale clause)	Cláusula a la vista (cláusula de vencimiento por venta)
Canons	Reglas
Capital gain	Ganancia de capital
Capitalize	Capitalizar
Cash flow	Flujo de efectivo
Cash value	Valor en efectivo
Cash-on-cash	Efectivo-sobre-efectivo
Caveat emptor	Caveat emptor (al riesgo del comprador)
CCR's (covenants, conditions, and restrictions)	CCR's (convenios, condiciones, y restricciones)
Certificate of deposit	Certificado de depósito
Certificate of occupancy	Certificado de tenencia
Chain of title	Cadena de título
Characteristics of land	Características de la tierra
Characteristics of value	Características de valor
Chattel	Bienes muebles
Chattel mortgage	Hipoteca de bienes muebles

Check	Check (medida de agrimensura)
Client	Cliente
Closing	Cierre
Closing date	Fecha de cierre
Closing into escrow	Cierre depositario
Closing meeting (settlement meeting)	Reunión de cierre
Cloud on the title	Nube sobre el título
Codicil	Codicilo
Color of title	Título aparente
Commingling	Mezclamiento
Common elements	Elementos comunes
Community property	Propiedad mancomunada
Community Reinvestment Act	Ley de reinversión en la comunidad
Comparables	Comparables
Compensation	Compensación
Competent parties	Partidos competentes
Competitive market analysis	Análisis del mercado competitivo
Computerized loan origination	Iniciación de préstamo computerizado
Condemnation proceeding	Procedimientos de condenación
Conditional sales contract. See installment contract	Contrato de venta condicional. Vea contrato a plazo
Conditional-use permit	Permiso de uso condicional
Condominium	Condominio
Condominium declaration	Declaración de condominio
Conformity, principle of	Principio de concordancia
Connection line	Línea de conexión
Consequential damages	Daños consecuentes
Consideration	Consideración
Construction loan (interim loan)	Préstamo para construcción (préstamo provisional)
Constructive eviction	Desalojo sobrentendido
Constructive notice	Notificación sobrentendida
Contour lines	Líneas de contorno
Contour map (topographic map)	Mapa de contornos (mapa topográfico)
Contract	Contrato

Contract for deed	Contrato por escritura
Contract rent	Renta contractual
Contractual intent	Intención del contrato
Contribution, principle of	Principio de contribución
Conventional loans	Préstamos convencionales
Cooperating broker	Corredor cooperativo
Cooperative	Cooperativa
Corporation	Corporación
Correction deed	Escritura de corrección
Correction lines	Líneas de corrección
Correlation process	Proceso de correlación
Cost approach	Método de costo
Counteroffer	Contraoferta
Covenant	Convenio
Covenant against encumbrances	Convenio contra gravamen
Covenant of seizin	Convenio de cesionista
Credit report	Informe de crédito
Curable depreciation	Depreciación curable
Curtesy	Propiedad raíz otorgada al viudo
Customers	Consumidores
Datum	Dato
Dedication	Dedicación
Deed	Escritura
Deed as security	Escritura como garantía
Deed of trust	Escritura de fideicomiso
Deed restrictions (deed covenants)	Restricciones de escritura (convenios de escritura)
Default	Incumplimiento
Defeasance clause	Cláusula resolutoria
Deficiency judgment	Fallo de deficiencia
Delayed exchange	Cambio demorado
Delinquent loan	Préstamo atrasado
Demand	Demanda
Depreciation	Depreciación
Dereliction	Terreno ganado por el receso del agua
Devise	Legado de bienes raíces
Devisee	Legatario
Diminishing marginal returns, principle of	Principio de regresos marginales decrecientes
Discount broker	Corredor de descuento

Discount points	Puntos de descuento
Discrimination. See Fair housing laws	Discriminación. Vea Leyes de Igualdad de Vivienda
Disintermediation	Falta de intermediación
Documentary tax	Impuesto sobre documentación
Dominant estate	Heredad dominante
Dower	Propiedad raíz otorgada a la viuda
Downside risk	Riesgo de pérdida
Downzoning	Cambio de zonificación
Dual agency (divided agency)	Agencia dual (agencia dividida)
Due-on-sale	Vencido con la venta
Durable power of attorney	Poder duradero
Duress	Coacción
Earnest money deposit	Depósito de buena fe
Easement	Servidumbre
Easement appurtenant	Servidumbre real
Easement by prescription	Servidumbre por prescripción
Easement in gross	Servidumbre personal
Economic obsolescence	Obsolescencia económica
Economic rent	Renta económica
Effective yield	Rendimiento efectivo
Emblements	Cosecha
Eminent domain	Dominio eminente
Encroachment	Intrusión
Encumbrance	Impedimento
Equitable mortgage	Hipoteca equitativa
Equitable title	Título equitativo
Equity	Valor líquido de propiedad
Equity build-up	Aumento del valor líquido de propiedad
Equity mortgage	Hipoteca a base del valor líquido de la propiedad
Equity of redemption	Derecho de redención
Equity sharing	Participación en adquisición
Escalation clause	Cláusula escalatoria
Escheat	Reversión al estado
Escrow account	Cuenta para depósitos en garantía

Escrow agent	Agente depositario
Escrow closing	Cierre depositario
Estate	Patrimonio
Estate at will	Posesión terminable
Estate for years	Posesión por años determinados
Estate in severalty	Propiedad en exclusive
Estoppel certificate	Certificado de impedimento
Exclusive agency listing	Contrato de venta de agencia exclusiva
Exclusive authority to purchase	Autoridad exclusiva de comprar
Exclusive right to sell	Derecho exclusivo para vender
Executor	Ejecutor testamentario
Executrix	Ejecutora testamentaria
Executor's deed	Escritura de ejecutor testamentario
Express contract	Contrato explícito
Face amount	Valor nominal
Fair Credit Reporting Act	Ley imparcial reportadora de Crédito
Fair Housing Laws	Leyes de Igualdad de Vivienda
Faithful performance	Fiel desempeño
Familial status	Estado familiar
Fannie Mae	Fannie Mae (Asociación Nacional Hipotecaria Federal)
Federal Home Loan Mortgage Corporation (Freddie Mac)	Corporación Federal de Préstamos Hipotecarios Para Viviendas (Freddie Mac)
Federal Housing Administration (FHA)	Administración Federal de Vivienda (FHA)
Federal National Mortgage Association (Fannie Mae)	Asociación Nacional Hipotecaria Federal (Fannie Mae)
Fee Simple	Pleno dominio
Fee simple determinable estate (fee on conditional limitation)	Pleno dominio de propiedad determinable (dominio con limitación condicional)
Fee simple subject condition subsequent	Pleno dominio sujeto a condición subsecuente

Fee simple upon condition precedent	Pleno dominio sobre condición precedente
Feudal system	Sistema feudal
Fiat money	Moneda fija
Fictional depreciation	Depreciación ficticia
Fiduciary	Fiduciario
Finance charge	Gasto financiero
Financial liability	Responsabilidad económica
Financing statement	Declaración de financiamiento
FIRREA (Financial Institutions Reform, Recovery, and Enforcement Act)	FIRREA (Ley de Reforma, Recuperación y Ejecución de Instituciones Financieras)
Fixity	Fijación
Fixture	Cosa fija
Flat-fee broker	Corredor de cobranza fija
Forbear	Abstener
Foreclosure	Procedimiento ejecutivo hipotecario
Formal will	Testamento formal
Four unities of joint tenancy	Los cuatro elementos de condominio
Franchise	Franquicia
Fraud	Fraude
Freddie Mac	Freddie Mac (Corporación Federal de Préstamos Hipotecarios Para Viviendas)
Freehold estate	Dominio absoluto de propiedad
Front foot	Pie frontal
Fructus industriales	Frutas industriales
Fructus naturales	Frutas naturales
Functional obsolescence	Obsolescencia funcional
Funding fee	Cuota de fondos
Fungible	Fungible
Gain	Ganancia
General agency	Agencia general
General lien	Gravamen general
General partnership	Sociedad colectiva
Gift deed	Escritura donativa
Ginnie Mae	Ginnie Mae (Asociación Gubernamental Hipotecaria Nacional)

Good consideration	Causa valiosa
Government National Mortgage Association (Ginnie Mae)	Asociación Gubernamental Hipotecaria Nacional (Ginnie Mae)
Government survey	Levantamiento gubernamental
Graduated payment mortgage	Hipoteca de pago graduado
Graduated rental	Arrendamiento graduado
Grant	Conceder
Grantee	Donatario
Grantor	Donador
Grantor-Grantee indexes	Índices de donador/donatario
GRM (Gross rent multiplier)	GRM (Multiplicador de alquiler bruto)
Gross lease	Alquiler bruto
Ground lease	Arrendamiento de terreno
Ground rent	Alquiler del terreno
Groundwater level	Nivel de agua subterránea
Guardian's deed	Escritura de guardián
Guide meridians	Guías meridianas
Handicapped	Personas incapacitadas
Heirs	Herederos
Highest and best use	Uso óptimo
Holdover tenant	Inquilino que retiene posesión
Holographic will	Testamento hológrafo
Home-seller program	Programa para el vendedor de hogar
Homestead protection	Protección del hogar principal
Hypothecate	Hipotecar
Illiquid asset	Bien ilíquido
Illiquidity	Falta de liquidez
Implied authority	Autorización Implícita
Implied contract	Contrato implícito
Impound or reserve account	Cuenta de reserva
Improvement district	Distrito de mejoras
Improvements	Mejoras
Income approach	Método de rendimiento por ingresos
Incurable depreciation	Depreciación incurable

Independent contractor	Contratista independiente
Index rate	Tasa índice
Indicated value	Valor indicado
Informal reference	Referencia informal
Innocent misrepresentation	Malinterpretación inocente
Installment contract	Contrato a plazo
Inter vivos trust	Fideicomiso entre vivos
Interest	Interés
Interest rate cap	Capa sobre tasa de interés
Interim loan	Préstamo interino
Intermediary	Intermediario
Intermediate theory	Teoría intermedia
Intestate	Intestado
Intestate succession	Sucesión intestada
Inverse condemnation	Condenación inversa
Investment strategy	Estrategia inversionista
Joint tenancy	Condominio
Joint venture	Empresa conjunta
Judgment roll	Expediente del juicio
Judicial foreclosure	Juicio hipotecario
Junior mortgage	Hipoteca subordinada
Jurat	Certificado de notario
Land patent	Patente de terreno, cesión de derechos
Land trust	Fideicomiso de terreno
Land-use control	Control sobre el uso de la tierra
Latitude lines	Líneas latitudinales
Lawful objective	Objetivo legítimo
Lease	Arrendamiento
Leasehold estate	Bienes forales
Lease-option	Arrendamiento con opción de compra
Legacy	Legado
Legal consideration	Causa lícita
Legatee	Legatario
Lessee	Arrendatario
Lessor	Arrendador
Leverage	Impacto de fondos prestados
License	Licencia
License revocation	Revocación de licencia

License suspensión	Suspensión de licencia
Licensee	Concesionario
Lien	Gravamen
Lien theory	Teoría de gravamen
Life estate	Dominio vitalicio
Life tenant	Propietario vitalicio
Limited common elements	Elementos comunes limitados
Limited liability company	Compañía de responsabilidad limitada
Limited partner	Socio limitado
Limited partnership	Sociedad limitada
Liquid asset	Activo líquido
Liquidated damages	Daños liquidados
Lis pendens	Litispendencia
Listing	Contrato para vender
Littoral right	Derecho litoral
Loan balance table	Tabla de saldo del préstamo
Loan escrow	Cuenta depositaria para pagar el préstamo
Loan origination fee	Cuota de iniciación de préstamo
Loan points	Puntos prestatarios
Loan servicing	Servicio prestatario
Loan value	Valor del préstamo
Loan-to-value ratio	Relación del préstamo al valor
Longitude lines	Líneas longitudinales
Loose money	Dinero desocupado
Loyalty to principle	Principio de lealtad
Maggie Mae	Maggie Mae (Corporación Aseguradora de Garantía Hipotecaria)
Maintenance fees	Cuotas de mantenimiento
Majority	Edad mayoritaria
Maker	Otorgante
Margin	Margen
Market approach	Método comparativo del mercado
Market value	Valor de Mercado
Marketable title	Título válido
Marketable title acts	Leyes sobre título válido
Master deed	Escritura maestra

Master limited partnership	Sociedad maestra limitada
Maturity	Vencimiento
Mechanic's lien	Gravamen mecánico
Meeting of the minds. See Mutual agreement	Acuerdo común. Vea Convenio mutuo
Menace	Amenaza
Meridian	Meridiano
Metes and bounds	Medidas y límites
MGIC (Mortgage Guarantee Insurance Corporation)	MGIC (Corporación Aseguradora de Garantía Hipotecaria)
Middleman	Intermediario
Mill rate	Tasa milésima
Minor, Infant	Menor, Infante
Misrepresentation. See Innocent misrepresentation	Malinterpretación. Vea Malinterpretación inocente
Mistake	Error
Modification	Modificación
Money damages	Daños monetarios
Monument	Monumento
Mortgage	Hipoteca
Mortgage banker	Banquero hipotecario
Mortgage broker	Corredor hipotecario
Mortgage company	Empresa hipotecaria
Mortgage insurance	Seguro hipotecario
Mortgage lien	Gravamen hipotecario
Mortgage pool	Consorcio de valores hipotecarios
Mortgage-backed security	Seguridades de respaldo hipotecario
Mortgagee	Acreedor hipotecario
Mortgagee's information letter	Carta informativa del acreedor hipotecario
Mortgagee's policy	Póliza hipotecaria
Mortgagor	Hipotecante
Mortgagor-mortgagee indexes	Índices hipotecante-hipotecario
Multiple listing service	Servicio múltiple de ventas
Municipal bond programs	Programa de bonos municipales
Mutual agreement	Convenio mutuo
Mutual rescission	Rescisión mutua

National Association of REALTORS® (NAR)	Asociación Nacional de Corredores
Negative amortization	Amortización negativa
Negative cash flow	Flujo de efectivo negativo
Negative leverage	Impacto negativo de dinero prestado
Net lease	Arrendamiento neto
Net listing	Contrato de venta de beneficio neto
Net operating income	Ingreso neto de operación
Net spendable	Neto disponible
Non-assumption clause	Cláusula de enajenación
Nonconforming use	Uso inconforme
Nonhomogeneity	Falta de homogeneidad
Nonjudicial foreclosure	Proceso hipotecario por el prestamista
Nonperforming loan	Préstamo incumplido
Notary public (In the U.S., this title is not equivalent to the position of notary public in Spanish-speaking countries.)	Notario público (En los EEUU, este título no es equivalente a la posición de notario en Iberoamérica.)
Note	Pagaré
Notice of consent	Noticia de consentimiento
Notice of revocation	Noticia de revocación
Novation	Novación
Nuncupative (oral) will	Testamento nuncupativo (oral)
Obedience (faithful performance)	Obediencia (cumplimiento fiel)
Offeree	Ofrecido
Offeror	Ofrecedor
Open listing	Contrato de venta abierto
Operating expense ratio	Relación de gastos operativos
Operating expenses	Gastos operativos
Opinion of title	Opinión de título
Option	Opción
Optionee	Tenedor de opción
Optioner	Concesionario de opción
Origination fee	Cuota de iniciación
Ostensible authority	Autoridad ostensible
Outside of escrow. See Outside of the closing	Fuera de depositario. Vea Fuera del cierre

Outside of the closing	Fuera del cierre
Overall rate	Tasa total
Overencumbered property	Propiedad excesivamente sobrecargada
Owner's policy	Póliza de propietario
Package mortgage	Hipoteca agrupada
Parol evidence rule	Regla de testimonio verbal
Partial release	Libertad parcial de hipotecaria
Partially amortized loan	Préstamo parcialmente amortizado
Participation certificate	Certificado de participación
Participation loan	Préstamo en participación
Partition	Partición
Partnership	Asociación copropietaria
Party (parties)	Partido (partidos)
Party wall easement	Pared servidumbre de los partidos
Payment cap	Capa de pagos
Percentage basis	Base sobre porcentaje
Percolating water	Agua al nivel freático
Performance	Cumplimiento
Periodic estate	Propiedad periódica
Personal property	Propiedad personal
Personalty	Bienes muebles
Physical deterioration	Deterioración física
PITI payment	Pago PITI (principal, interés, impuestos, seguro)
Planned unit development	Desarrollo de unidades planeado
Plat	Plano
Plottage value	Aumento de valor
Point	Punto
Point of beginning	Punto de inicio
Police power	Fuerza pública
Positive cash flow	Flujo de efectivo positivo
Positive leverage	Impacto positivo de fondos prestados
Power of attorney	Carta de personería
Power of sale	Poder de venta
Prepayment penalty	Multa por pago adelantado

Prepayment privilege	Privilegio de pago adelantado
Prescriptive easement	Servidumbre por prescripción
Price fixing	Fijación de precios
Primary market	Mercado Primario
Principal	Principal
Principal meridian	Meridiano principal
Principles of value	Principios de valor
Private mortgage insurance	Seguro hipotecario privativo
Pro forma statement	Declaración pro forma
Probate court	Tribunal testamentario
Procuring cause	Causa próxima
Projected gross	Proyectado bruto
Promissory note	Pagaré
Proprietary lease	Arrendamiento por el propietario
Prorating	Prorratear
Prospectus	Prospecto
Public grant	Concesión pública
Public improvement	Mejora pública
Puffing	Exageración
Pur autre vie	Por la vida de otro
Purchase money mortgage	Hipoteca por parte del precio de compra
Qualified fee estate	Posesión de dominio limitada
Quarter-section	Un cuarto de una sección
Quiet enjoyment	Quieta y pacífica posesión
Quiet title suit	Demanda titular
Quitclaim deed	Escritura de finiquito
Ready, willing, and able buyer	Comprador listo, dispuesto y capaz
Real chattel	Bien real
Real estate	Bienes raíces
Real estate commission	Comisión de Bienes Raíces
Real estate commissioner	Comisionado de bienes raíces
Real estate investment trust	Fideicomiso de inversiones bienes raíces
Real estate lien note	Nota gravamen de bienes raíces

Real estate listing. See Listing	Contrato de venta de bienes raíces. Vea Contrato de venta
Real Estate Settlement Procedure Act	Ley Sobre Procedimientos del Cierre en Bienes Raíces
Real property	Propiedad raíz
Real savings	Ahorros reales
REALTOR®	Corredor
REALTOR®-associate	Asociado del corredor
Realty	Propiedad inmueble
Reasonable care	Prudencia razonable
Reciprocity	Reciprocidad
Recorded map. See Recorded plat	Mapa registrado. Vea plano registrado
Recorded plat	Plano registrado
Recorded survey. See Recorded plat	Levantamiento registrado. Vea plano registrado
Recording acts	Leyes de registro
Recovery fund	Fondo de recuperación
Rectangular survey system	Sistema de levantamiento rectangular
Redlining	Redlining (rechazo de préstamos)
Regular mortgage	Hipoteca ordinaria
Regulation Z	Reglamento Z (mostrar el costo de crédito)
Release of lien	Exoneración de gravamen
Reliction (dereliction)	Terreno ganado
Remainder interest	Interés restante
Remainderman	Nudo propietario
Rental value	Valor de arriendo
Replacement cost	Costo de reposición
Replacement value	Valor de reposición
Reproduction cost	Costo de reproducción
Reserve account	Cuenta de reserva
Reserves for replacement	Reservas para reemplazo
Resort timesharing	Sitio furístico de tiempo compartido
RESPA (Real Estate Settlement Procedure Act)	Ley sobre procedimientos del cierre de bienes raíces
Restrictive covenants	Convenios restrictivos
Reverse mortgage	Hipoteca inversa
Reverse-annuity mortgage	Hipoteca de anualidad inversa

Reversionary interest	Interés de reversión
Right of first refusal	Derecho de primera opción
Right of survivorship	Derecho de supervivencia
Riparian right	Derechos ribereños
S Corporation	Corporación S
Sale and leaseback	Venta y arriendo inverso
Sale by advertisement	Venta por anuncio
Sales associate	Socio de ventas
Salesperson	Vendedor
Salvage value	Valor de salvamento
Scheduled gross (projected gross)	Renta bruta proyectada (proyectado bruto)
Secondary mortgage market	Mercado hipotecario secundario
Section	Sección
Seller financing	Financiamiento por el vendedor
Seller's affidavit of title	Declaración del vendedor sobre el título
Seller's market	Mercado de vendedor
Senior mortgage	Hipoteca primaria
Separate property	Propiedad separada
Servient estate	Predio sirviente
Settlement	Cierre
Settlement statement	Declaración de cierre
Severalty ownership	Pertenencia exclusiva
Severance damages	Daños de parcelación
Sheriff's deed	Escritura judicial
Situs	Situs (sitio)
Sole ownership	Pertenencia exclusiva
Special agency	Agencia especial
Special assessment	Tasación especial
Special warranty deed	Escritura de garantía especial
Specific lien	Gravamen específico
Specific performance	Cumplimiento específico
Specific property offering	Ofrecimiento de propiedad específica
Spot zoning	Zonificación esporádica
Square-foot method	Método de pie cuadrado
Standard mortgage	Hipoteca uniforme
Standard of parallel	Paralelo uniforme
Statute of Frauds	Ley sobre fraudes

Statute of limitations	Estatuto de limitaciones
Statutory estates	Bienes estatuarios
Steering	Conducción
Step-up rental	Arrendamiento graduado
Straight-line depreciation	Depreciación linear
Subject property	Propiedad sujeta
Subject to an existing loan	Sujeto al préstamo existente
Sublease	Subarriendo
Sublessee	Subarrendatario
Sublessor	Subarrendador
Subordination	Subordinación
Substitution, principle of	Principio de substitución
Subsurface right	Derecho subterráneo
Sunk cost	Costo incurrido
Surface rights	Derechos de superficie
Survey books	Registro de levantamientos
Survivorship, right of	Derecho de supervivencia
Syndication (syndicate)	Sindicación (sindicato financiero)
Tack on	Aumentación de ocupación
Take-out loan	Préstamo permanente
Taking back paper	Pagaré por efectivo
Tax basis	Base imponible
Tax lien	Gravamen de impuestos
Tax shelter	Protector de impuestos
Tax–deferred exchange	Cambio para diferir impuesto
Teaser rate	Tasa incitadora
Tenancy at sufferance	Posesión por tolerancia
Tenancy by the entirety	Tenencia en totalidad, vitalicia
Tenancy in common	Tenientes en común
Tenant	Teniente
Term loan	Préstamo de término
Testamentary trust	Fideicomiso testamentario
Testate	Testado
Testator (testatrix)	Testador (testadora)
Tester	Comprobador
Thin market	Mercado de poca actividad
Third parties	Terceros

Tight money	Crédito escaso
Time is of the essence	El tiempo es de esencia
Timesharing	Tiempo compartido
Title	Título
Title by descent	Título por descendencia
Title by prescription. See Adverse possession	Título por prescripción. Vea prescripción adquisitiva
Title closing	Traspaso del título
Title cloud	Nube sobre título
Title commitment	Compromiso de título
Title insurance	Seguro de título
Title search	Investigación de título
Title theory	Teoría de título
Total payments	Pagos totales
Townships	Sexmos
Tract index	Índice de terrenos
Trade fixture	Mueble adherido comercial
Trigger terms	Términos causantes de reacciones impulsivas
Trust	Fideicomiso
Trust account	Cuenta fiduciaria
Trust deed. See Deed of trust	Escritura fiduciaria. Vea Escritura de Fideicomiso
Trustee	Fiduciario
Trustee's deed. See Sheriff's deed	Escritura de fiduciario. Vea Escritura judicial
Trustor	Fideicomitente
Truth-in-Lending Act	Ley de Veracidad en Préstamos
U.S. Public Lands Survey	Levantamiento de los Terrenos Públicos de los Estados Unidos
UCC lien	Gravamen de Código Comercial Uniforme
Undivided interest	Interés indiviso
Undue influence	Influencia excesiva
Unenforceable contract	Contrato inejecutable
Unilateral contract	Contrato unilateral
Unilateral rescission	Rescisión unilateral
Unit deed	Escritura de unidad
Unity of interest	Unidad de interés
Unity of person	Unidad de persona

Unity of possession	Posesión conjunta
Unity of time	Unidad de tiempo
Unity of title	Unidad de título
Universal agency	Agencia universal
Up-front mortgage insurance Premium	Prima anticipada de seguro hipotecario
Urban homestead	Hogar principal urbano
Usury	Usura
Utility	Utilidad
VA	Administración de Veteranos
Valid contract	Contrato válido
Valuabe consideration	Consideración valiosa
Valuation of real property. See Appraisal	Valuación de bienes raíces. Vea Avalúo
Variable rate mortgage	Hipoteca de tasa variable
Variance	Variancia
Vassals	Vasallos
Vendee	Comprador
Vendor	Vendedor
Vested	Propio
Void Contract	Contrato inválido
Voidable contract	Contrato anulable
Voluntary lien	Gravamen voluntario
Walk-through	Inspección final
Warranty	Garantía
Warranty deed	Escritura con garantía de título
Waste	Desperdicio
Water right	Derecho de agua
Water table	Nivel hidrostático
Words of conveyance	Palabras de cesión
Worst-case scenario	Escenario del peor caso
Wraparound mortgage	Hipoteca circundante subordinada
Writ of Execution	Mandato de ejecución
Zoning	Zonificación

Spanish-English Key

Abstener	Forbear
Abstractor	Abstractor
Accesión	Accession
Acre	Acre
Acrecencia	Accretion
Acreedor hipotecario	Mortgagee
Activo líquido	Liquid asset
Acuerdo común. Vea Convenio mutuo	Meeting of the minds. See Mutual agreement
Administración de Veteranos	VA
Administración Federal de Vivienda (FHA)	Federal Housing Administration (FHA)
Administrador (administradora)	Administrator (administratrix)
Agencia	Agency
Agencia aunada a un interés	Agency coupled with an interest
Agencia dual (agencia dividida)	Dual agency (divided agency)
Agencia especial	Special agency
Agencia general	General agency
Agencia por impedimento	Agency by estoppel
Agencia por ratificación	Agency by ratification
Agencia universal	Universal agency
Agente	Agent
Agente depositario	Escrow agent
Agrupación	Assemblage
Agua al nivel freático	Percolating water
Ahorros reales	Real savings
Alquiler bruto	Gross lease
Alquiler del terreno	Ground rent
Aluvión	Alluvion
Amenaza	Menace
Amortización negativa	Negative amortization
Análisis del mercado competitivo	Competitive market analysis
Apoderado	Attorney-in-fact
Apreciación	Appreciation
Arrendamiento	Lease
Arrendamiento con opción de compra	Lease-option
Arrendamiento de terreno	Ground lease

Arrendamiento graduado	Graduated rental
Arrendamiento graduado	Step-up rental
Arrendamiento neto	Net lease
Arrendamiento por el propietario	Proprietary lease
Arrendador	Lessor
Arrendatario	Lessee
Asociación	Association
Asociación copropietaria	Partnership
Asociación Gubernamental Hipotecaria Nacional (Ginnie Mae)	Government National Mortgage Association (Ginnie Mae)
Asociación Nacional de Corredores	National Association of REALTORS® (NAR)
Asociación Nacional Hipotecaria Federal (Fannie Mae)	Federal National Mortgage Association (Fannie Mae)
Asociado del corredor	REALTOR®-associate
Aumentación de ocupación	Tack on
Aumento de valor	Plottage value
Aumento del valor líquido de propiedad	Equity build-up
Autoridad exclusiva de comprar	Exclusive authority to purchase
Autoridad ostensible	Ostensible authority
Autorización Implícita	Implied authority
Avaluar	Appraise
Avalúo	Appraisal
Avulsión	Avulsion
Bancos	Banks
Banquero hipotecario	Mortgage banker
Base	Basis
Base imponible	Tax basis
Base sobre porcentaje	Percentage basis
Beneficiario	Beneficiary
Bien ilíquido	Illiquid asset
Bien real	Real chattel
Bienes estatuarios	Statutory estates
Bienes forales	Leasehold estate
Bienes muebles	Chattel
Bienes muebles	Personalty
Bienes raíces	Real estate
Boicot	Boycotting
Cadena de título	Chain of title
Cambio de zonificación	Downzoning

Cambio demorado	Delayed exchange
Cambio para diferir impuesto	Tax–deferred exchange
Cantidad financiada	Amount financed
Cantidad realizada	Amount realized
Capa de pagos	Payment cap
Capa sobre tasa de interés	Interest rate cap
Capitalizar	Capitalize
Características de la tierra	Characteristics of land
Características de valor	Characteristics of value
Carta de avalúo	Appraisal letter
Carta de personería	Power of attorney
Carta informativa del acreedor hipotecario	Mortgagee's information letter
Causa lícita	Legal consideration
Causa próxima	Procuring cause
Causa valiosa	Good consideration
Caveat emptor (al riesgo del comprador)	Caveat emptor
CCR's (convenios, condiciones, y restricciones)	CCR's (covenants, conditions, and restrictions)
Ceder	Assign
Certificado de depósito	Certificate of deposit
Certificado de impedimento	Estoppel certificate
Certificado de notario	Jurat
Certificado de participación	Participation certificate
Certificado de tenencia	Certificate of occupancy
Cesión	Assignment
Cesionario	Assignee
Check (medida de agrimensura)	Check
Cierre	Closing
Cierre	Settlement
Cierre depositario	Closing into escrow
Cierre depositario	Escrow closing
Cláusula a la vista (cláusula de vencimiento por venta)	Call clause (due on sale clause)
Cláusula de enajenación	Alienation clause
Cláusula de enajenación	Non-assumption clause
Cláusula escalatoria	Escalation clause

Cláusula resolutoria	Defeasance clause
Cliente	Client
Coacción	Duress
Codicilo	Codicil
Comisión de Bienes Raíces	Real estate commission
Comisionado de bienes raíces	Real estate commissioner
Como está	As-is
Compañía de responsabilidad limitada	Limited liability company
Comparables	Comparables
Compendio	Abstract
Compendio del título	Abstract of Title
Compensación	Compensation
Comprador	Vendee
Comprador listo, dispuesto y capaz	Ready, willing, and able buyer
Comprobador	Tester
Compromiso de título	Title commitment
Conceder	Grant
Concesión pública	Public grant
Concesionario	Licensee
Concesionario de opción	Optioner
Condenación inversa	Inverse condemnation
Condominio	Condominium
Condominio	Joint tenancy
Conducción	Steering
Consideración	Consideration
Consideración valiosa	Valuabe consideration
Consorcio a ciegas	Blind pool
Consorcio de valores hipotecarios	Mortgage pool
Consumidores	Customers
Contraoferta	Counteroffer
Contratista independiente	Independent contractor
Contrato	Contract
Contrato a plazo	Installment contract
Contrato anulable	Voidable contract
Contrato bilateral	Bilateral contract
Contrato de venta abierto	Open listing

Contrato de venta condicional. Vea contrato a plazo	Conditional sales contract. See installment contract
Contrato de venta de agencia exclusiva	Exclusive agency listing
Contrato de venta de beneficio neto	Net listing
Contrato de venta de bienes raíces. Vea Contrato de venta	Real estate listing. See Listing
Contrato explícito	Express contract
Contrato implícito	Implied contract
Contrato inejecutable	Unenforceable contract
Contrato inválido	Void Contract
Contrato para vender	Listing
Contrato por escritura	Contract for deed
Contrato unilateral	Unilateral contract
Contrato válido	Valid contract
Control sobre el uso de la tierra	Land-use control
Convenio	Covenant
Convenio contra gravamen	Covenant against encumbrances
Convenio de cesionista	Covenant of seizin
Convenio de venta. Vea contrato a plazo	Agreement of sale. See installment contract
Convenio mutuo	Mutual agreement
Convenios restrictivos	Restrictive covenants
Cooperativa	Cooperative
Corporación	Corporation
Corporación Federal de Préstamos Hipotecarios Para Viviendas (Freddie Mac)	Federal Home Loan Mortgage Corporation (Freddie Mac)
Corporación S	S Corporation
Corredor	Broker
Corredor	REALTOR®
Corredor cooperativo	Cooperating broker
Corredor de cobranza fija	Flat-fee broker
Corredor de descuento	Discount broker
Corredor hipotecario	Mortgage broker
Corredor representante del comprador	Buyer's broker
Cosa fija	Fixture
Cosecha	Emblements

Costo de reposición	Replacement cost
Costo de reproducción	Reproduction cost
Costo incurrido	Sunk cost
Crédito escaso	Tight money
Cuenta de reserva	Impound or reserve account
Cuenta de reserva (cuenta de depósito)	Reserve account (impound account)
Cuenta depositaria para pagar el préstamo	Loan escrow
Cuenta fiduciaria	Trust account
Cuenta para depósitos en garantía	Escrow account
Cumplimiento	Performance
Cumplimiento específico	Specific performance
Cuota de fondos	Funding fee
Cuota de iniciación	Origination fee
Cuota de iniciación de préstamo	Loan origination fee
Cuotas de asociación	Association dues
Cuotas de mantenimiento	Maintenance fees
Daños consecuentes	Consequential damages
Daños de parcelación	Severance damages
Daños liquidados	Liquidated damages
Daños monetarios	Money damages
Dato	Datum
Declaración de cierre	Settlement statement
Declaración de condominio	Condominium declaration
Declaración de financiamiento	Financing statement
Declaración del vendedor sobre el título	Seller's affidavit of title
Declaración pro forma	Pro forma statement
Dedicación	Dedication
Demanda	Demand
Demanda titular	Quiet title suit
Depósito de buena fe	Earnest money deposit
Depreciación	Depreciation
Depreciación acelerada	Accelerated depreciation
Depreciación curable	Curable depreciation
Depreciación ficticia	Fictional depreciation
Depreciación incurable	Incurable depreciation
Depreciación linear	Straight-line depreciation
Derecho aéreo	Air right

Derecho de agua	Water right
Derecho de primera opción	Right of first refusal
Derecho de redención	Equity of redemption
Derecho de supervivencia	Right of survivorship
Derecho de supervivencia	Survivorship, right of
Derecho exclusivo para vender	Exclusive right to sell
Derecho litoral	Littoral right
Derecho subterráneo	Subsurface right
Derechos de superficie	Surface rights
Derechos ribereños	Riparian right
Desalojo sobrentendido	Constructive eviction
Desarrollo de unidades planeado	Planned unit development
Desperdicio	Waste
Deterioración física	Physical deterioration
Deuda hipotecaria	Purchase money mortgage
Dinero desocupado	Loose money
Discriminación. Vea Leyes de Igualdad de Vivienda	Discrimination. See Fair Housing Laws
Distrito avaluado. Vea Distrito de mejoras	Assessed district. See Improvement district
Distrito de mejoras	Improvement district
Documento de venta	Bill of sale
Dominio absoluto de propiedad	Freehold estate
Dominio eminente	Eminent domain
Dominio vitalicio	Life estate
Donador	Grantor
Donatario	Grantee
Edad mayoritaria	Majority
Efectivo-sobre-efectivo	Cash-on-cash
Ejecutor testamentario	Executor
Ejecutora testamentaria	Executrix
El tiempo es de esencia	Time is of the essence
Elementos comunes	Common elements
Elementos comunes limitados	Limited common elements
Empresa conjunta	Joint venture
Empresa hipotecaria	Mortgage company
Empresa localizadora de apartamentos	Apartment locators
En riesgo	At risk

Enajenación de título	Alienation of title
Error	Mistake
Escenario del peor caso	Worst-case scenario
Escritura	Deed
Escritura como garantía	Deed as security
Escritura con garantía de título	Warranty deed
Escritura de compraventa	Bargain and sale deed
Escritura de corrección	Correction deed
Escritura de ejecutor testamentario	Executor's deed
Escritura de fideicomiso	Deed of trust
Escritura de fiduciario. Vea Escritura judicial	Trustee's deed. See Sheriff's deed
Escritura de finiquito	Quitclaim deed
Escritura de garantía especial	Special warranty deed
Escritura de guardián	Guardian's deed
Escritura de unidad	Unit deed
Escritura donativa	Gift deed
Escritura fiduciaria. Vea Escritura de Fideicomiso	Trust deed. See Deed of trust
Escritura judicial	Sheriff's deed
Escritura maestra	Master deed
Estado familiar	Familial status
Estatuto de limitaciones	Statute of limitations
Estatutos	Bylaws
Estrategia inversionista	Investment strategy
Exageración	Puffing
Exoneración de gravamen	Release of lien
Expediente del juicio	Judgment roll
Fallo de deficiencia	Deficiency judgment
Falta de homogeneidad	Nonhomogeneity
Falta de intermediación	Disintermediation
Falta de liquidez	Illiquidity
Fannie Mae (Asociación Nacional Hipotecaria Federal)	Fannie Mae
Fecha de cierre	Closing date
Fideicomiso	Trust
Fideicomiso de inversiones bienes raíces	Real estate investment trust (REIT)

Fideicomiso de terreno	Land trust
Fideicomiso entre vivos	Inter vivos trust
Fideicomiso testamentario	Testamentary trust
Fideicomitente	Trustor
Fiduciario	Fiduciary
Fiduciario	Trustee
Fiel desempeño	Faithful performance
Fijación	Fixity
Fijación de precios	Price fixing
Financiamiento por el vendedor	Seller financing
FIRREA (Ley de Reforma,Recuperación y Ejecución de Instituciones Financieras)	FIRREA (Financial Institutions Reform, Recovery, and Enforcement Act)
Flujo de efectivo	Cash flow
Flujo de efectivo negativo	Negative cash flow
Flujo de efectivo positivo	Positive cash flow
Fondo de recuperación	Recovery fund
Fraude	Fraud
Freddie Mac (Corporación Federal de Préstamos Hipotecarios Para Viviendas)	Freddie Mac
Franquicia	Franchise
Frutas industriales	Fructus industriales
Frutas naturales	Fructus naturales
Fuera de depositario. Vea Fuera del cierre	Outside of escrow. See Outside of the closing
Fuera del cierre	Outside of the closing
Fuerza pública	Police power
Fungible	Fungible
Ganancia	Gain
Ganancia de capital	Capital gain
Garantía	Warranty
Gasto financiero	Finance charge
Gastos operativos	Operating expenses
Ginnie Mae (Asociación Gubernamental Hipotecaria Nacional)	Ginnie Mae
Gravamen	Lien

Gravamen de Código Comercial Uniforme	UCC lien
Gravamen de impuestos	Tax lien
Gravamen específico	Specific lien
Gravamen general	General lien
Gravamen hipotecario	Mortgage lien
Gravamen mecánico	Mechanic's lien
Gravamen voluntario	Voluntary lien
GRM (Multiplicador de alquiler bruto)	GRM (Gross rent multiplier)
Guías meridianas	Guide meridians
Heredad dominante	Dominant estate
Herederos	Heirs
Hipoteca	Mortgage
Hipoteca a base del valor líquido de la propiedad	Equity mortgage
Hipoteca agrupada	Package mortgage
Hipoteca circundante subordinada	Wraparound mortgage
Hipoteca colectiva	Blanket mortgage
Hipoteca con tasa ajustable	Adjustable rate mortgage
Hipoteca de anualidad inversa	Reverse-annuity mortgage
Hipoteca de bienes muebles	Chattel mortgage
Hipoteca de pago graduado	Graduated payment mortgage
Hipoteca de tasa variable	Variable rate mortgage
Hipoteca en segundo grado	Second mortgage
Hipoteca equitativa	Equitable mortgage
Hipoteca integrada con activo	Asset integrated mortgage
Hipoteca inversa	Reverse mortgage
Hipoteca módica	Budget mortgage
Hipoteca ordinaria	Regular mortgage
Hipoteca primaria	Senior mortgage
Hipoteca subordinada	Junior mortgage
Hipoteca uniforme	Standard mortgage
Hipotecante	Mortgagor

Hipotecar	Hypothecate
Hogar principal urbano	Urban homestead
Impacto de fondos prestados	Leverage
Impacto negativo de dinero prestado	Negative leverage
Impacto positivo de fondos prestados	Positive leverage
Impedimento	Encumbrance
Impuesto sobre documentación	Documentary tax
Impuestos al valor	Ad valorem taxes
Incumplimiento	Default
Incumplimiento del contrato	Breach of contract
Índice de terrenos	Tract index
Índices de donador/ donatario	Grantor-Grantee indexes
Índices hipotecante- hipotecario	Mortgagor-mortgagee indexes
Influencia excesiva	Undue influence
Informe de crédito	Credit report
Ingreso neto de operación	Net operating income
Iniciación de préstamo computerizado	Computerized loan origination
Inquilino que retiene posesión	Holdover tenant
Inspección del comprador	Buyer's walk-through
Inspección final	Walk-through
Intención del contrato	Contractual intent
Interés	Interest
Interés beneficial	Beneficial Interest
Interés de reversión	Reversionary interest
Interés indiviso	Undivided interest
Interés restante	Remainder interest
Intermediario	Intermediary
Intermediario	Middleman
Intestado	Intestate
Intrusión	Encroachment
Investigación de título	Title search
Juicio hipotecario	Judicial foreclosure
Junta revisora de avalúos	Appraisal review board
Legado	Bequest

Nivel de agua subterránea	Groundwater level
Nivel hidrostático	Water table
Nota gravamen de bienes raíces	Real estate lien note
Notario público (En los EEUU, este título no es equivalente a la posición de notario en Iberoamérica.)	Notary public (In the U.S., this title is not equivalent to the position of notary public in Spanish-speaking countries.)
Noticia de consentimiento	Notice of consent
Noticia de revocación	Notice of revocation
Notificación efectiva	Actual notice
Notificación sobrentendida	Constructive notice
Novación	Novation
Nube sobre el título	Cloud on the title
Nube sobre título	Title cloud
Nudo propietario	Remainderman
Obediencia (cumplimiento fiel)	Obedience (faithful performance)
Objetivo legítimo	Lawful objective
Obsolescencia económica	Economic obsolescence
Obsolescencia funcional	Functional obsolescence
Ofrecedor	Offeror
Ofrecido	Offeree
Ofrecimiento de propiedad específica	Specific property offering
Opción	Option
Opinión de título	Opinion of title
Otorgante	Maker
Pagaré	Note
Pagaré	Promissory note
Pagaré por efectivo	Taking back paper
Pago de saldo mayor	Balloon payment
Pago PITI (principal, interés,impuestos,seguro)	PITI payment
Pagos totales	Total payments
Palabras de cesión	Words of conveyance
Paralelo uniforme	Standard of parallel
Pared servidumbre de los partidos	Party wall easement
Partición	Partition
Participación en adquisición	Equity sharing

Partido (partidos)	Party (parties)
Partidos competentes	Competent parties
Patente de terreno, cesión de derechos	Land patent
Patrimonio	Estate
Permiso de uso condicional	Conditional-use permit
Personas incapacitadas	Handicapped
Pertenencia	Appurtenance
Pertenencia exclusiva	Sole ownership
Pertenencia exclusiva	Severalty ownership
Pie frontal	Front foot
Plano	Plat
Plano registrado	Recorded plat
Pleno dominio	Fee Simple
Pleno dominio de propiedad determinable (dominio con limitación condicional)	Fee simple determinable estate (fee on conditional limitation)
Pleno dominio sobre condición precedente	Fee simple upon condition precedent
Pleno dominio sujeto a condición subsecuente	Fee simple subject condition subsequent
Poder de venta	Power of sale
Poder duradero	Durable power of attorney
Póliza de propietario	Owner's policy
Póliza hipotecaria	Mortgagee's policy
Por la vida de otro	Pur autre vie
Posesión conjunta	Unity of possession
Posesión de dominio limitada	Qualified fee estate
Posesión por años determinados	Estate for years
Posesión por tolerancia	Tenancy at sufferance
Posesión terminable	Estate at will
Precio ajustado del mercado	Adjusted market price
Precio de venta ajustado	Adjusted sales price
Predio sirviente	Servient estate
Prescripción adquisitiva	Adverse possession
Préstamo adquirido	Assumed loan
Préstamo amortizado	Amortized loan
Préstamo atrasado	Delinquent loan
Préstamo de saldo mayor	Balloon loan

Préstamo de taza combinada	Blended-rate loan
Préstamo de término	Term loan
Préstamo en participación	Participation loan
Préstamo incumplido	Nonperforming loan
Préstamo interino	Interim loan
Préstamo para construcción(préstamo provisional)	Construction loan (interim loan)
Préstamo parcialmente amortizado	Partially amortized loan
Préstamo permanente	Take-out loan
Préstamos convencionales	Conventional loans
Prima anticipada de seguro hipotecario	Up-front mortgage insurance Premium
Principal	Principal
Principio de anticipación	Anticipation, principle of
Principio de concordancia	Conformity, principle of
Principio de contribución	Contribution, principle of
Principio de lealtad	Loyalty to principal
Principio de regresos marginales decrecientes	Diminishing marginal returns, principle of
Principio de substitución	Substitution, principle of
Principios de valor	Principles of value
Privilegio de pago adelantado	Prepayment privilege
Procedimientos de condenación	Condemnation proceeding
Proceso de apropiación	Appropriation process
Proceso de correlación	Correlation process
Proceso hipotecario por el prestamista	Nonjudicial foreclosure
Programa de bonos municipales	Municipal bond programs
Programa para el vendedor de hogar	Home-seller program
Propiedad mancomunada	Community property
Propiedad en exclusiva	Estate in severalty
Propiedad excesivamente sobrecargada	Overencumbered property
Propiedad inmueble	Realty
Propiedad periódica	Periodic estate
Propiedad personal	Personal property

Propiedad raíz	Real property
Propiedad raíz otorgada a la viuda	Dower
Propiedad raíz otorgada al viudo	Curtesy
Propiedad separada	Separate property
Propiedad sujeta	Subject property
Propietario vitalicio	Life tenant
Propio	Vested
Prorratear	Prorating
Prospecto	Prospectus
Protección del hogar principal	Homestead protection
Protector de impuestos	Tax shelter
Provisión para vencimiento anticipado	Acceleration clause
Proyectado bruto	Projected gross
Prudencia razonable	Reasonable care
Punto	Point
Punto de inicio	Point of beginning or point of commencement
Punto de referencia	Benchmark
Puntos de descuento	Discount points
Puntos de prestatario	Borrower's points
Puntos prestatarios	Loan points
Quieta y pacífica posesión	Quiet enjoyment
Reciprocidad	Reciprocity
Reconocimiento	Acknowledgment
Redlining (rechazo de préstamos)	Redlining
Referencia informal	Informal reference
Registro de avalúos	Assessment roll
Registro de levantamientos	Survey books
Regla de testimonio verbal	Parol evidence rule
Reglamento Z (mostrar el costo de crédito)	Regulation Z
Reglamentos de construcción	Building codes
Reglas	Canons
Relación de gastos operativos	Operating expense ratio
Relación del préstamo al valor	Loan-to-value ratio
Rendimiento efectivo	Effective yield

Renta bruta proyectada (proyectado bruto)	Scheduled gross (projected gross)
Renta contractual	Contract rent
Renta económica	Economic rent
Rescisión mutua	Mutual rescission
Rescisión unilateral	Unilateral rescission
Reservas para reemplazo	Reserves for replacement
Responsabilidad económica	Financial liability
Restricciones de escritura (convenios de escritura)	Deed restrictions (deed covenants)
Reunión de cierre	Closing meeting (settlement meeting)
Reversión al estado	Escheat
Revocación de licencia	License revocation
Riesgo de pérdida	Downside risk
Rompe cuadras	Blockbusting
Sección	Section
Seguridades de respaldo hipotecario	Mortgage-backed security
Seguro de título	Title insurance
Seguro hipotecario	Mortgage insurance
Seguro hipotecario privativo	Private mortgage insurance
Servicio múltiple de ventas	Multiple listing service
Servicio prestatario	Loan servicing
Servidumbre	Easement
Servidumbre personal	Easement in gross
Servidumbre por prescripción	Easement by prescription
Servidumbre por prescripción	Prescriptive easement
Servidumbre real	Easement appurtenant
Sexmos	Townships
Sindicación (sindicato financiero)	Syndication (syndicate)
Sistema alodial	Allodial system
Sistema automático de subscripción	Automated underwriting systems
Sistema de levantamiento rectangular	Rectangular survey system
Sistema feudal	Feudal system
Sitio furístico de tiempo compartido	Resort timesharing

Situs (sitio)	Situs
Sociedad colectiva	General partnership
Sociedad limitada	Limited partnership
Sociedad maestra limitada	Master limited partnership
Socio de ventas	Sales associate
Socio limitado	Limited partner
Subarrendador	Sublessor
Subarrendatario	Sublessee
Subarriendo	Sublease
Subordinación	Subordination
Sucesión intestada	Intestate succession
Sujeto al préstamo existente	Subject to an existing loan
Suspensión de licencia	License suspensión
Tabla de saldo del préstamo	Loan balance table
Tasa de porcentaje anual	Annual percentage rate
Tasa incitadora	Teaser rate
Tasa índice	Index rate
Tasa milésima	Mill rate
Tasa total	Overall rate
Tasación especial	Special assessment
Tenedor de opción	Optionee
Tenencia en totalidad, vitalicia	Tenancy by the entirety
Teniente	Tenant
Tenientes en común	Tenancy in common
Teoría de gravamen	Lien theory
Teoría de título	Title theory
Teoría intermedia	Intermediate theory
Terceros	Third parties
Términos causantes de reacciones impulsivas	Trigger terms
Terreno ganado	Reliction (dereliction)
Terreno ganado por el receso del agua	Dereliction
Testado	Testate
Testador (testadora)	Testator (testatrix)
Testamento formal	Formal will
Testamento hológrafo	Holographic will
Testamento nuncupativo (oral)	Nuncupative (oral) will
Tiempo compartido	Timesharing
Título	Title

Título aparente	Color of title
Título equitativo	Equitable title
Título por descendencia	Title by descent
Título por prescripción. Vea prescripción adquisitiva	Title by prescription. See Adverse possession
Título válido	Marketable title
Traspaso del título	Title closing
Tribunal testamentario	Probate court
Un cuarto de una sección	Quarter-section
Unidad de interés	Unity of interest
Unidad de persona	Unity of person
Unidad de tiempo	Unity of time
Unidad de título	Unity of title
Uso inconforme	Nonconforming use
Uso óptimo	Highest and best use
Usura	Usury
Utilidad	Utility
Valor catastral	Assessed Value
Valor de arriendo	Rental value
Valor de Mercado	Market value
Valor de reposición	Replacement value
Valor de salvamento	Salvage value
Valor del préstamo	Loan value
Valor en efectivo	Cash value
Valor indicado	Indicated value
Valor líquido de propiedad	Equity
Valor nominal	Face amount
Valuación de bienes raíces. Vea Avalúo	Valuation of real property. See Appraisal
Valuador	Appraiser
Variancia	Variance
Vasallos	Vassals
Vencido con la venta	Due-on-sale
Vencimiento	Maturity
Vendedor	Salesperson
Vendedor	Vendor
Venta por anuncio	Sale by advertisement
Venta y arriendo inverso	Sale and leaseback
Zona amortiguadora	Buffer zone
Zonificación	Zoning
Zonificación esporádica	Spot zoning

Directory of Major Real Estate Trade Associations, Publications, Data Resources, and Web Site Addresses

Below is a list of online resources starting with trade associations, publications, directories and data resource Web sites organized by functional area or resource type. Please be aware that some links may become defunct over time.

TRADE ASSOCIATIONS

AACA – American Association of Certified Appraisers

AIA – American Institute of Architects

AI – Appraisal Institute

AIC – Appraisal Institute of Canada

A.I.R. – American Industrial Real Estate Association

ARES – American Real Estate Society

AREUEA – American Real Estate-Urban Economics Association

ASA – American Society of Appraisers

ASHI – American Society of Home Inspectors

ATA – American Land Title Association

APA – American Planning Association

AUREO – Association of University Real Estate Officials

BOMA – Building Owners and Managers Association

CCIM – Commercial Investment Real Estate Institute

CORENet – New Organization of Corporate Real Estate based on the combination of IDRC and NACORE as described below

CRE – American Society of Real Estate Counselors

EAA – Environment Assessment Association

ERES – European Real Estate Society

EuroFM – European Facilities Management Network

FIABCI – International Real Estate Federation

HDB – Housing and Development Board

HIF – Housing Inspection Foundation

HMBA – Hotel and Motel Brokers of America

Homer Hoyt Institute – a post doctorate real estate school and leading real estate think tank based in North Palm Beach Florida.

IAAO – International Association of Assessment Officers

ICSC – International Council of Shopping Centers

IDRC (USA) – International Development Research Council

IDRC (CANADA) – International Development Research Centre

IREC – Institutional Real Estate Clearinghouse

IREI – Institute of Real Estate

IREM – Institute of Real Estate Management

LAI – Lambda Alpha International

MBAA – Mortgage Bankers Association of America

Multifamily Housing Institute

NACORE – International Association of Corporate Real Estate Executives

NAHB – National Association of Home Builders

NAHRO – National Association of Housing and Redevelopment Officials

NAIOP – National Association of Industrial and Office Parks

NAR – National Association of REALTORS®

NAREA – National Association of Real Estate Appraisers

NICA – National Independent Contractors Association

NAREIA – National Real Estate Investors Association

NAREIT – National Association of Real Estate Investment Trusts

NARPM – National Association of Residential Property Managers

NCREIF – National Council of Real Estate Investment Fiduciaries

NMHC – National Multi Housing Council

NNCREW – National Commercial Real Estate Women

PCA – Property Council of Australia

PREA – Pension Real Estate Association

PRRES – Pacific Rim Real Estate Society

RECRA – Real Estate Capital Resources Association

REEA – Real Estate Educators Association

RIN – National Association of REALTORS®

RERI – Real Estate Research Institute

RICS – The Royal Institution of Chartered Surveyors (United Kingdom Property Appraisers)

R/W – International Right of Way Association

SIOR – Society of Industrial REALTORS®

ULI – Urban Land Institute

URA – Urban Redevelopment Authority

PUBLICATIONS DIRECTORY
Academic Journals

Real Estate Economics (AREUEA):
www.areuea.org

Journal of Property Investment and Finance:
www.emeraldinsight.com/jpif.htm

Journal of Real Estate Practice and Education:
www.aresnet.org/ARES/pubs/jrepe/JREPE.html

Journal of Real Estate Literature:
www.aresnet.org/ARES/pubs/jrel/JREL.html

Journal of Real Estate Portfolio Management:
www.aresnet.org/ARES/pubs/jrepm/JREPM.html

Journal of Real Estate Research (JRER):
www.aresnet.org/ARES/pubs/jrer/JRER.html

REITnet online: www.reitnet.com/realsource

Professional and Private Publications

Crittenden Publishers specializing in real estate finance and leasing: www.crittendenonline.com/

Institutional Real Estate, Inc. offering a series of institutionally oriented newsletters and magazines, including electronic versions such as IREIzine: www.ire-net.com

Urban Land published by the Urban Land Institute: www.uli.org

Development published by NAIOP: www.naiop.org

Shopping Centers Today published by the ICSC:
www.icsc.org

RESOURCES AND WEB SITES
Jobs and Resume Posting
www.real-jobs.com

Residential Listings and Homeownership
www.iown.com

www.homestore.com

www.realtor.org

www.nareb.com

Elected Officials
State and loal representatives: www.statelocal.gov

Mayors: www.usmayors.org

Counties: www.naco.org

Cities: www.nlc.org

Community Development, Support Groups and Public Housing
The Enterprise Foundation:
www.enterprisefoundation.org

Local initiatives support: www.liscnet.org

Housing and Redevelopment Officials:
www.nahro.org

African American Housing: www.noaah.org

Rural housing assistance: www.ruralhome.org

Homeless assistance: www.endhomelessness.org
and http://www.nationalhomeless.org/

The Urban League: www.nul.org

Center for Community Change:
www.communitychange.org

Property, Tenant and Construction Data
The CoStar Group of property and tenant data:
www.costargroup.com

Torto-Wheaton: www.tortowheaton.com

REIS: www.reis.com

Loopnet: www.loopnet.com

The Data Consortium: www.dataconsortium.com

National Real Estate Index: www.realestateindex.com

NAI Commercial Reports: www.naidirect.com

Demographics, Employment and Population Trends

The best free government site: www.census.gov

GeoVue mapping and data firm:
www.geonomicsinc.com

Wessex data and maps: www.wessex.com

Donnelley data: www.donnelleymarketing.com

Equifax reports including credit and profiles:
www.equifax.com

Bureau of Labor Statistics: www.bls.gov

Woods and Poole market research:
www.woodsandpoole.com

Property Tax Data

E-property Tax: www.epropertytax.com

Natural Hazards Data

National Geophysical Data Center (NGDC):
www.ngdc.noaa.gov

Brokerage/Listings for Lease or Sale

National sale/lease site: www.loopnet.com

Data and listings: www.costargroup.com

Space with aerial views: www.officespace.com

Retail: www.storetrax.com

www.excessspace.com

www.offices2Share.com

Serving brokers: www.tenantwise.com

Brokerage/Leasing Support

Software, resources, and links for financing
and marketing: www.myrealestateoffice.com

Converts faxes to e-mails, saves paper:
www.efax.com

ePad by interlink for online signature support:
http://www.interlinkelec.com/

Commercial Financing Web Sites

www.capitalthinking.com

www.mortgageramp.com (mortgage brokerage)

New Construction and Project Management Support

Monitoring for architects, engineers, contractors:
www.Citadon.co

Viewing drawings online: www.buzzsaw.com
and www.e-builder.com

Direct supplies oriented toward home builders:
www.USBUILD.com

Green Building

Green Building Products:
www.greenguide.com/about.html

Green building resources:
www.eeba.org/sites/green.htm

Green Building: *A Primer for builders,
consumers and Realtors*:
www.nrg-builder.com/greenbld.htm

Checklist for Environmentally Responsible
Design and Construction:
www.buildinggreen.com/ebn/checklist.html

Green Building, construction techniques and
estimates: www.greenhome.org/

Mold

EPA's Mold Resource Site:
www.epa.gov/iaq/molds/moldresources.html

The Indoor Air Quality Association resources:
www.iaqa.org/mold_resources.htm

Insurance industry: http://www.moldupdate.com/

National Association of Home Builders:
www.moldtips.com/

Source: Miller, Norman and Geltner, David, *Real Estate
Principles for the New Economy*. Cincinnati, OH: South-
Western Publishing. 2003. Reprinted with permission.